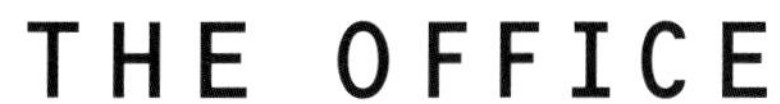
THE OFFICE

THE OFFICE

Steven Ahlgren

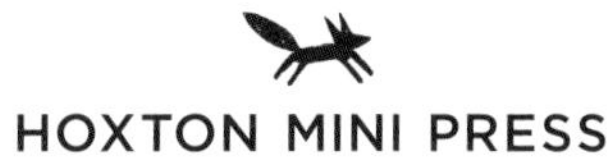

HOXTON MINI PRESS

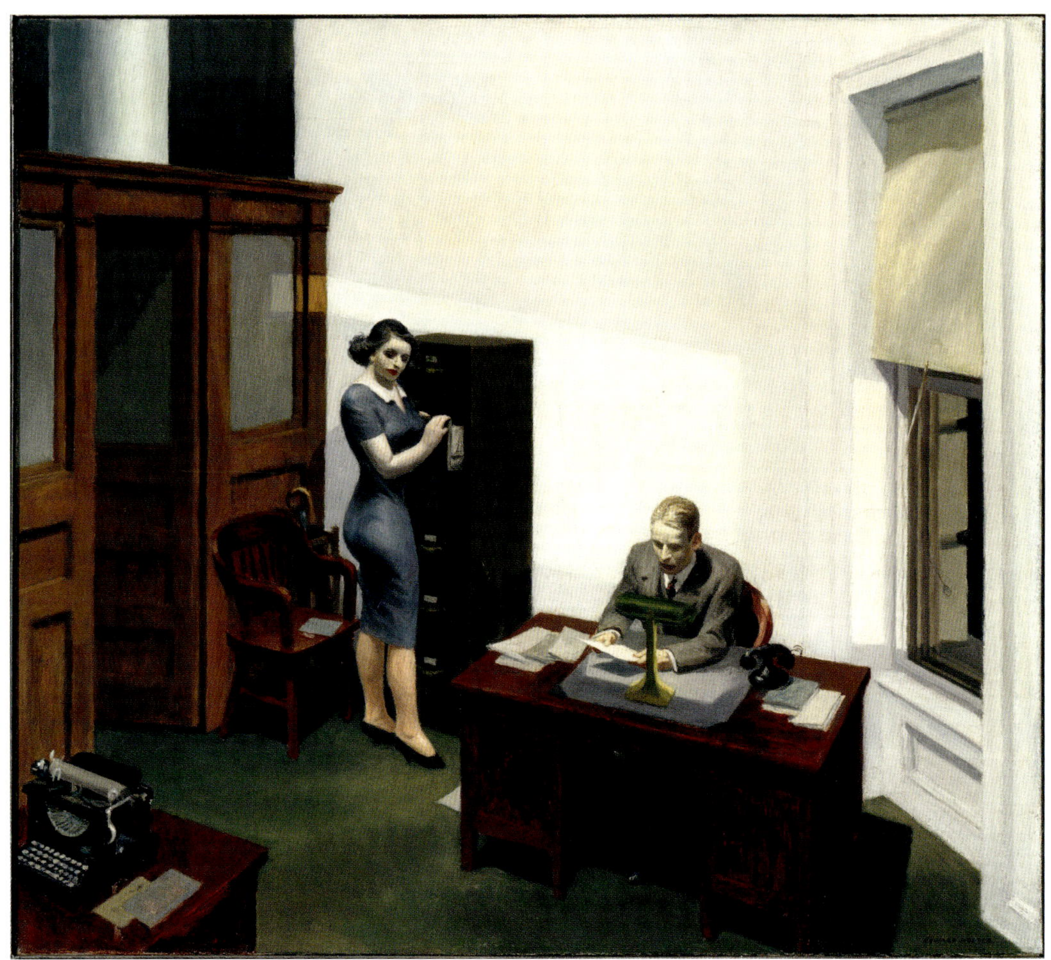

Edward Hopper, *Office at Night* (1940)

MY WORK AT THE OFFICE
Steven Ahlgren

In 1987, when I was bored and unfulfilled working as a banker in Minneapolis,
I began taking frequent trips to the Walker Art Center to look at a painting by
Edward Hopper, *Office at Night*. What probably first drew me to the picture was
its setting, which I related to each and every workday at the bank. But what kept
pulling me back over time was its ambiguous narrative - who were these two
individuals, what was their relationship, and why was the woman looking at
that piece of paper on the floor? I was far more excited thinking about Hopper's
picture of this office than about any work I had to attend to in my own.

As I gradually became more interested in photography and less interested
in banking, I began to notice scenes around me that seemed quietly evocative,
and reminded me of Hopper's paintings. When working late I was fascinated by how
the light in some empty offices and corridors appeared almost theatrical. In
meetings, my attention would occasionally drift from the matter at hand, and I
would observe the subtle expressions and gestures of those around me. Sometimes
I saw that what was being discussed had profound consequences - professional and
personal - for others in the room, although their emotions were usually veiled
by professional decorum.

It wasn't until later, when I'd left banking for graduate school to study photography, that I went into an office with a camera to try and portray some of these ideas. I eventually worked at this project for about ten years, between 1990 and 2001, in a variety of offices but always with the same approach: nothing would be staged and only the light that was available would be used.

Even though I am no longer working on this project, I am reminded of it every time I enter an office building, or overhear a fragment of conversation about office life: a promotion won or lost, the challenges of beginning at a new firm, a difficult relationship with a superior or subordinate. Sometimes, afterwards, I remember these conversations and try to imagine how the moment described would have looked as a picture.

***

INTRODUCTION

Ufrieda Ho

Back in the days before work-from-home became an acronym, when we dressed up not just for what the laptop camera could see, we worked in actual offices. We also actually *went* to work.

Steven Ahlgren's photographs document this office of the not-so-distant past, reminding us that our workdays once started with a swipe of our security cards and a shove through turnstiles to join a human surge towards waiting metal elevators. Our clocked-in days, deadlines met and targets nailed were recorded on whiteboards and flipcharts, then magically transformed into paid bills and buoyed hopes of year-end bonuses.

But office life has always been about more than work. The office contains our second life, a world where we can escape for a while the worries of home: the hamster's skin rash, the rising damp inching up the dining-room walls.

Ahlgren's images show that in the office, we got to put our best feet forwards, even when they'd been wearily dragged there. His images capture the curated versions of ourselves we presented: ironed shirts and ties, shoulder pads and styled hair. In the office, we understood our roles, routines and rituals, and we understood that looking and playing the part helped.

His photos draw us into familiar cubicles and glass-fronted rooms. There are the desks tidy and achingly bare, bar an in-tray and a tangle of computer cables. And there are the ones crammed with certificates, gimmicky figurines and a 'proper' lamp from home - casting a glow over polystyrene cups half filled with long-cooled coffee.

In this office, we got to free our competitive drive. We could argue points convincingly in a boardroom - speaking to the ghosts of CEOs past, frozen in identical frames on bland walls. Office interactions turned bright ideas into incandescent brilliance, or saw them fizzle as mere distractions from the monotony of same ol', same ol' reports needing to get done. Our work-worth was constantly tested or affirmed, refracted through our bosses, our contemporaries and, especially, those colleagues who we were glad stayed in the boundaries of our nine-to-five. They were the ones who made every 'quick' meeting a 90-minute talked-up turnaround strategy. And when their grandstanding got the boss's nodding enthusiasm, it signalled to us that we'd be staying logged in long after the desks around us had cleared for after-work drinks. We'd be playing catch up with only the lonely burble from the water cooler for inspiration and companionship.

But under the endless array of cold, fluorescent tube lights, we also found the people we liked to eat lunch with; the colleagues whose birthdays we celebrated by dangling paper balloons, inked with happy messages, from the backing-board ceilings above their desks. There might have been singing too, followed by slices of cake served up on sheets of photocopier paper.

The office made us a work tribe; we belonged. We were together in a space marked off by wiry-carpeted square metres and a time marked off by the same clock, counting down to the workday's end. We were bound by a certainty that, come the next workday, we would gather once more and do it all over again.

Our Covid-recalibrated world hushed the hum of office life, turning memories into nostalgia. But Ahlgren's images, made over a decade, stir them from their silence. Some things will not have survived in the offices we return to - briefcases, shoulder pads, that neglected plant. But other things will be exactly as they've always been. Mismatched office chairs with wonky casters will still roll around boardrooms. Colleagues will still leave uneaten apples to oxidise behind computer monitors. And the pieces of tinsel from five Christmases ago will still be flapping from the air vent - it will feel like we never left at all.

* * *

Insurance Company

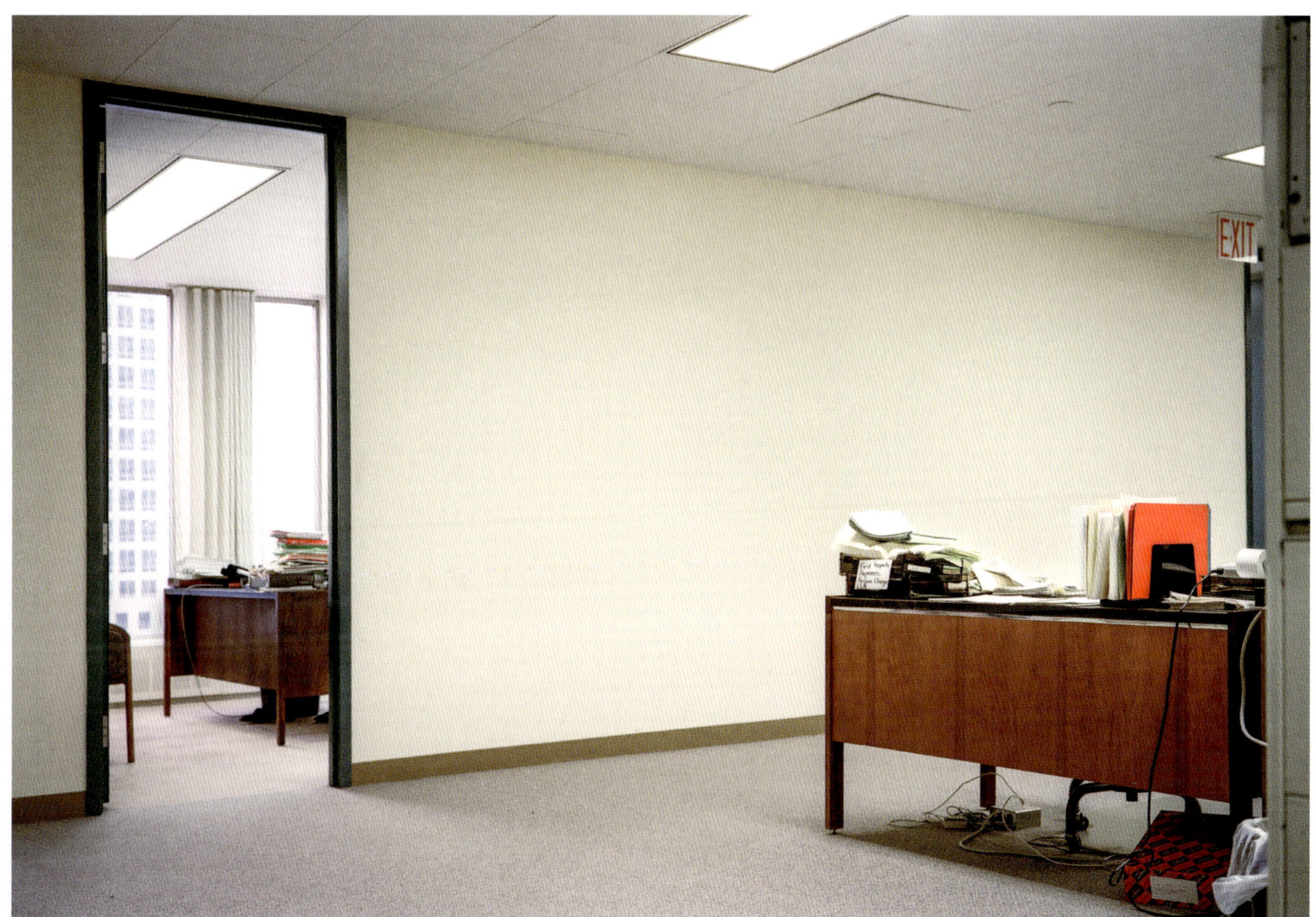

EXIT

Savings and Loan Company

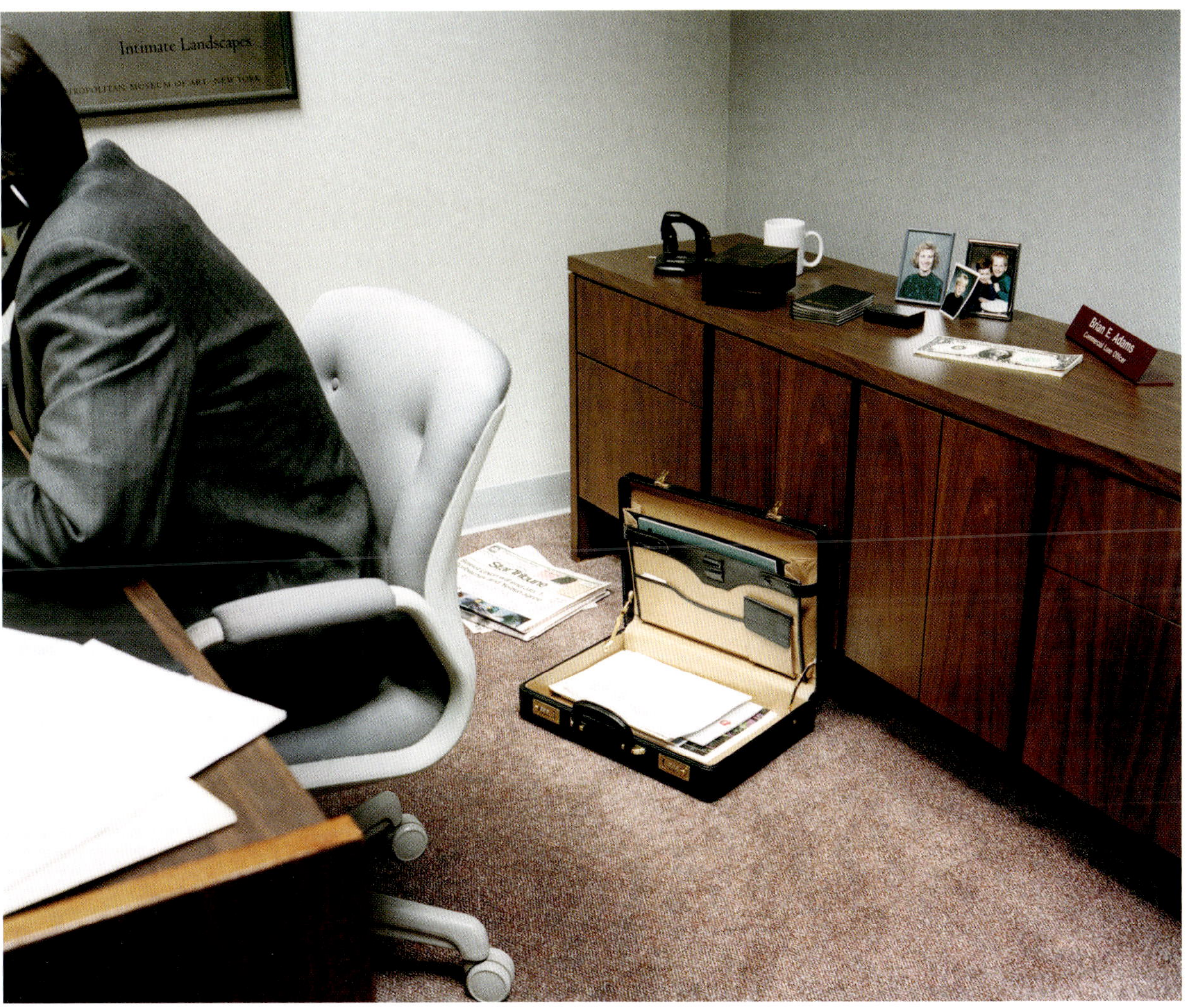

Intimate Landscapes
METROPOLITAN MUSEUM OF ART · NEW YORK
Brian E. Adams
Commercial Loan Officer

Law Firm

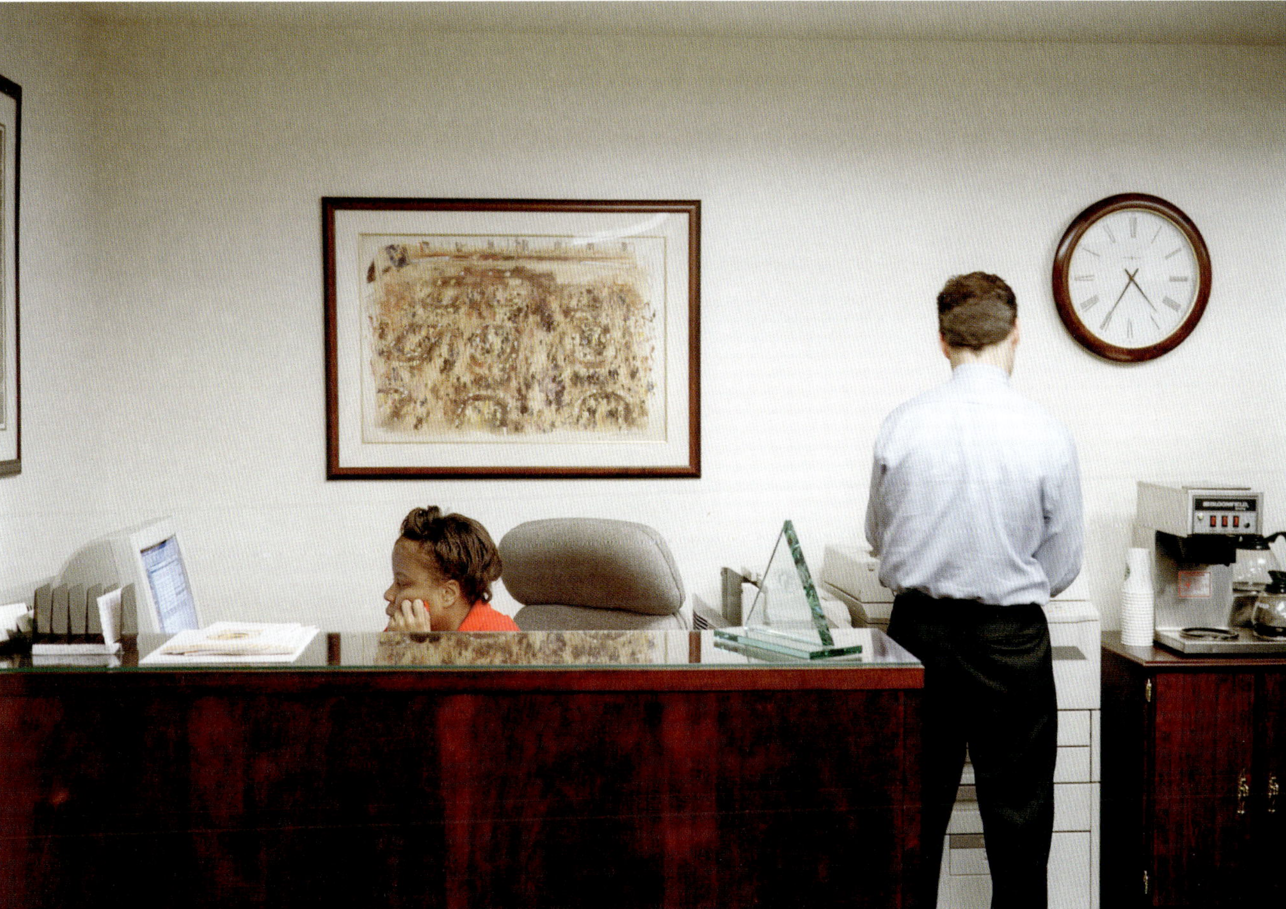

Financial Advisory Firm

overleaf: Law Firm *(left),* Commercial Bank *(right)*

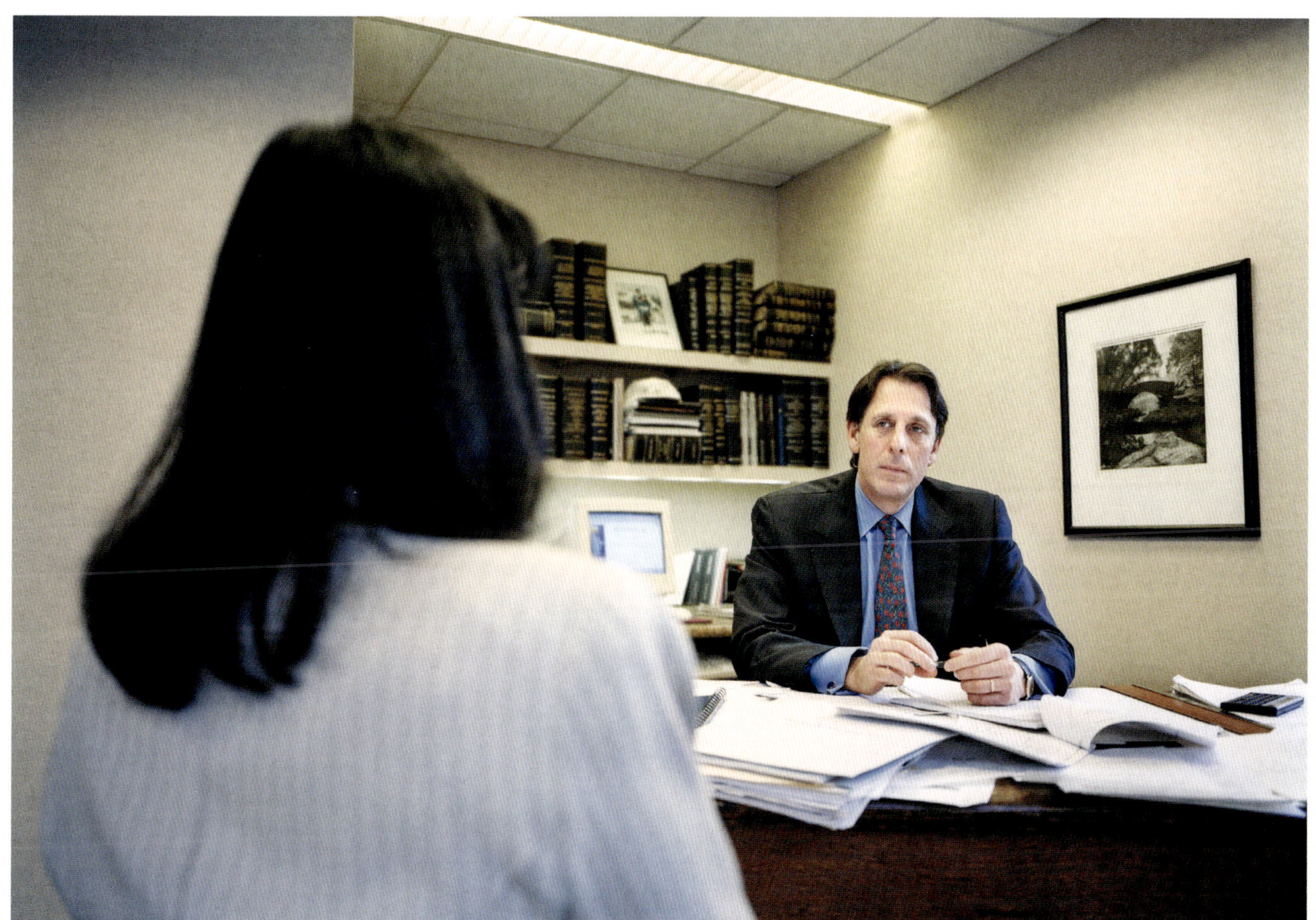

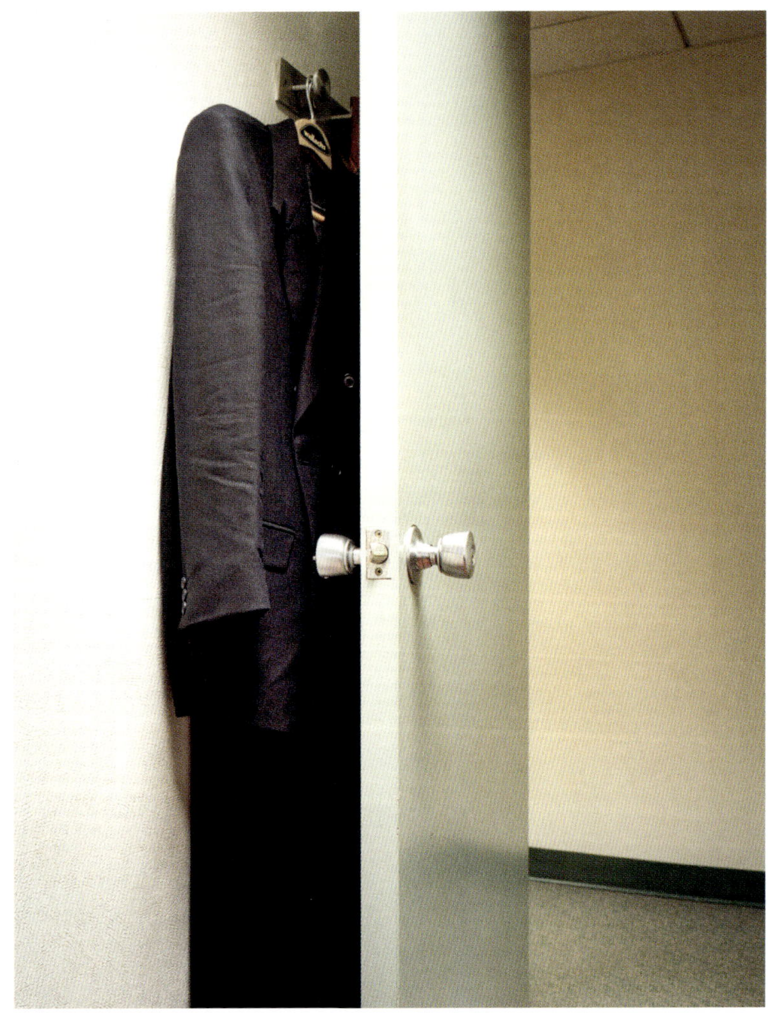

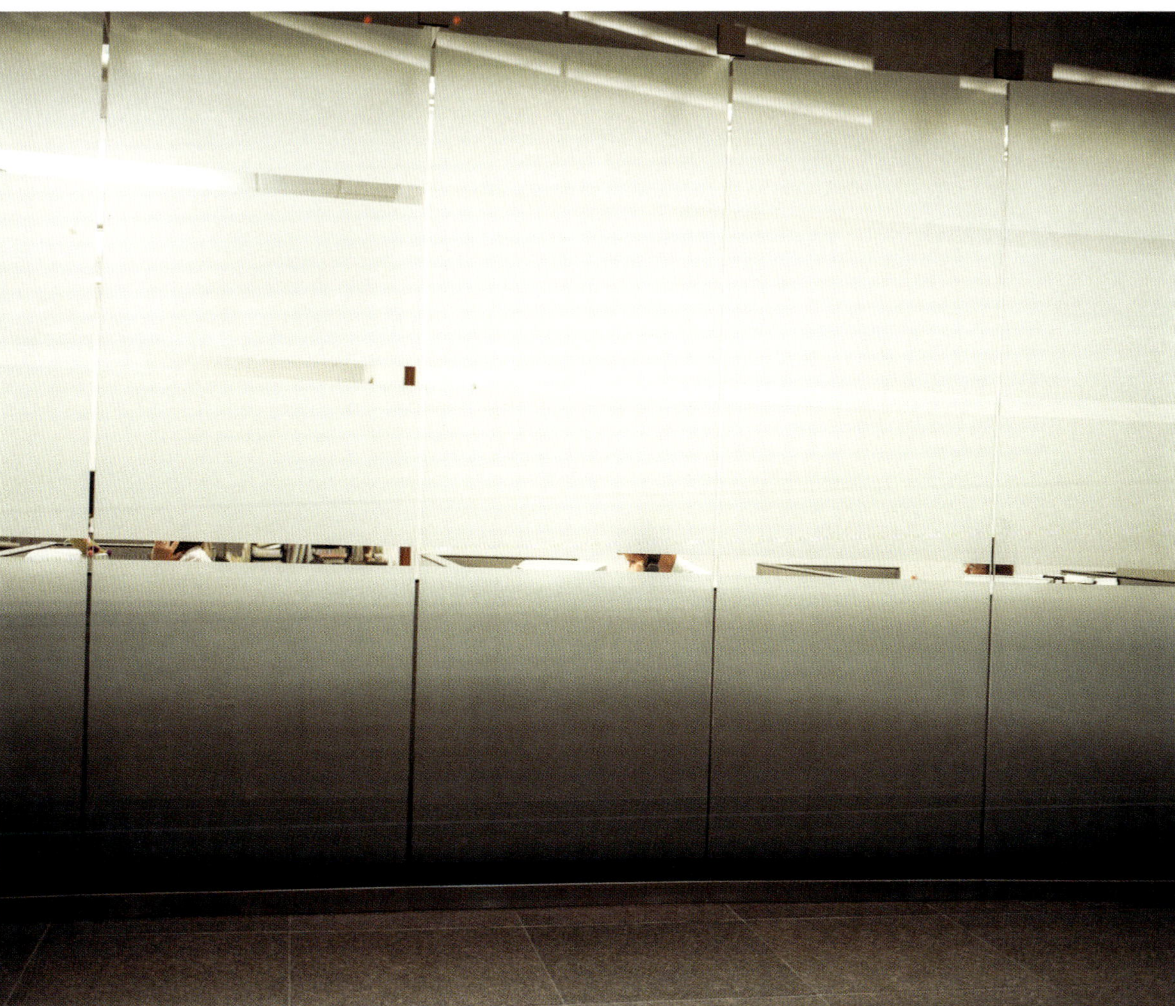

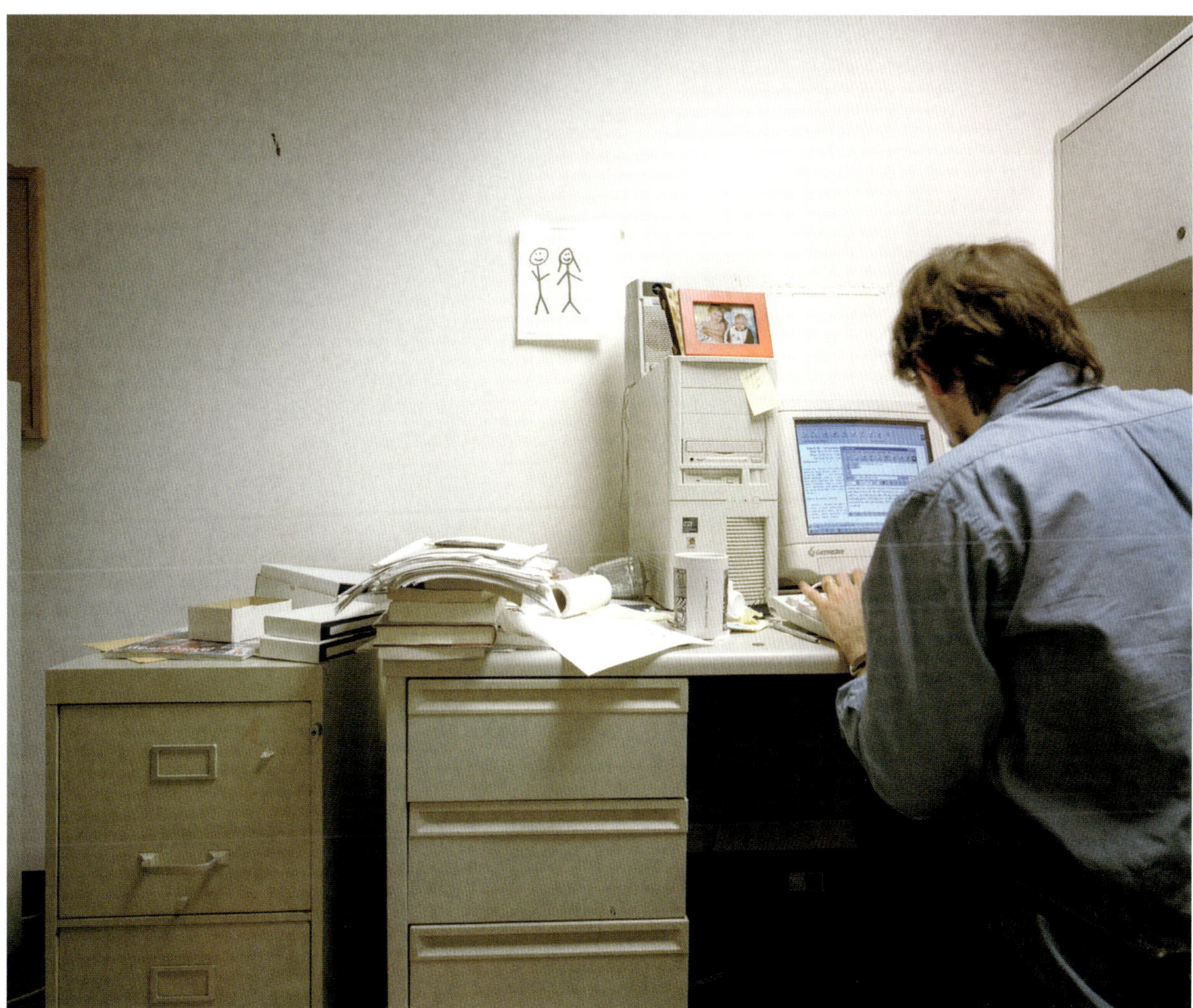

Accounting Firm

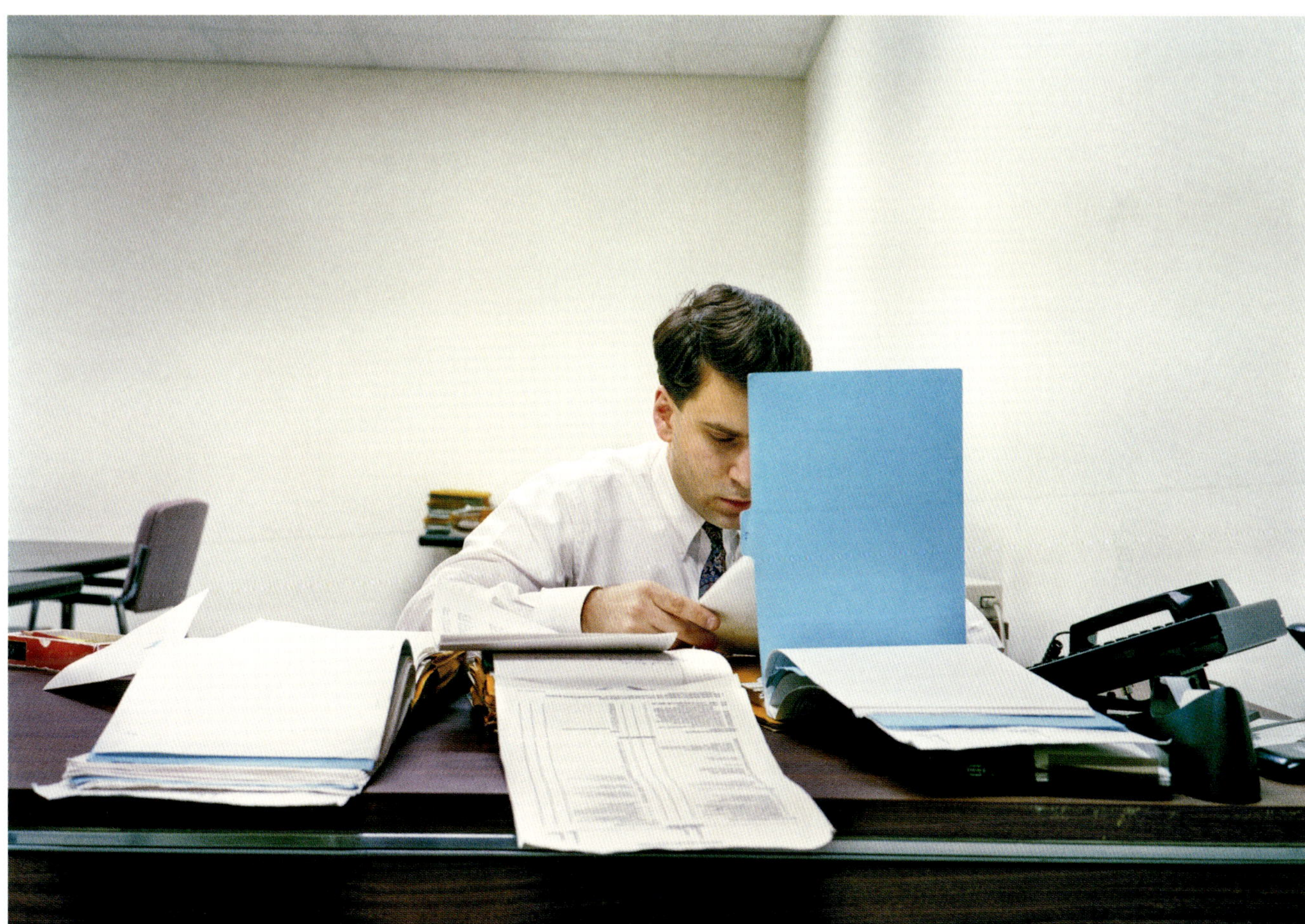

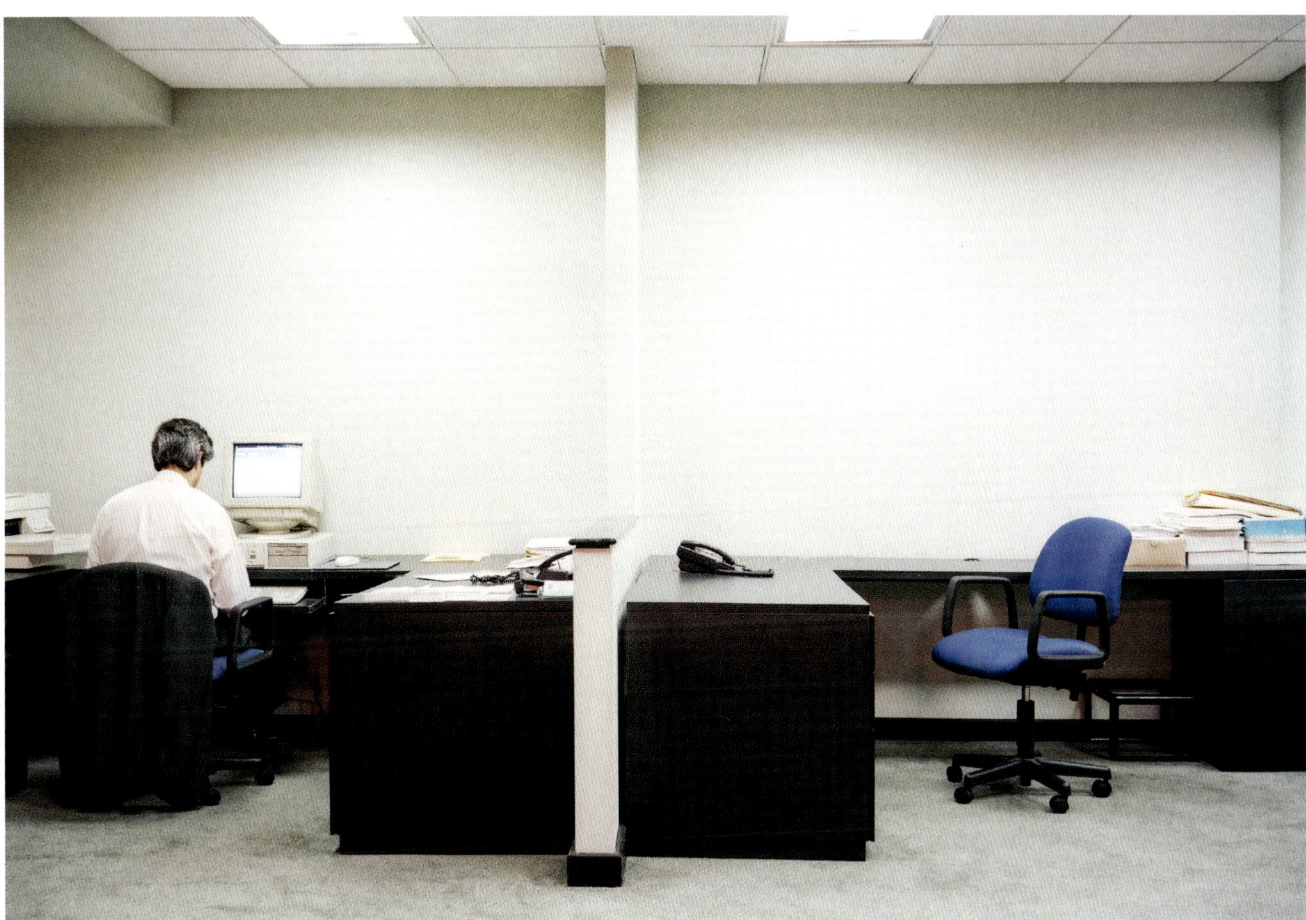

Insurance Company

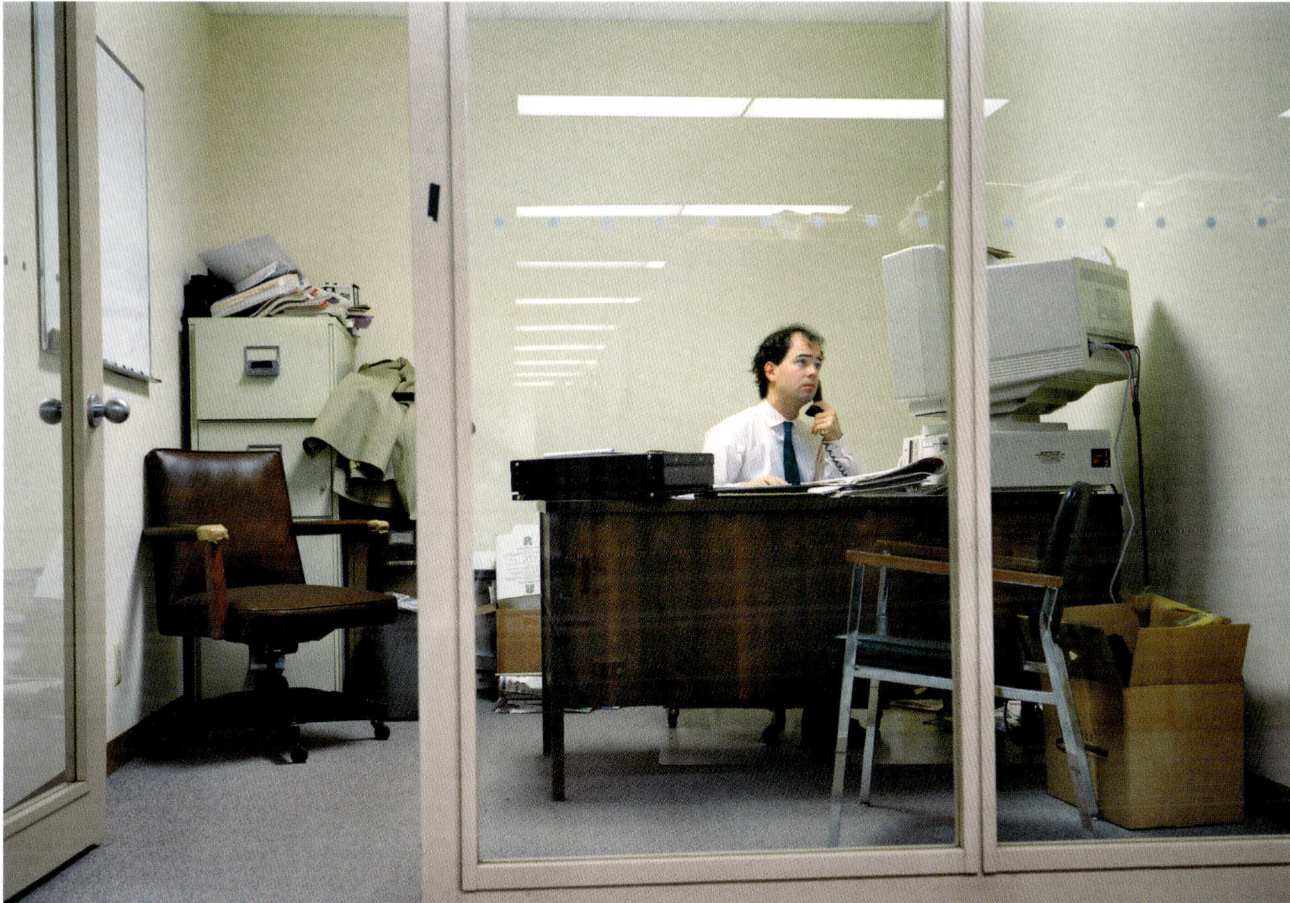

Insurance Company

overleaf: Telephone Company *(left),* Office Furniture Manufacturer *(right)*

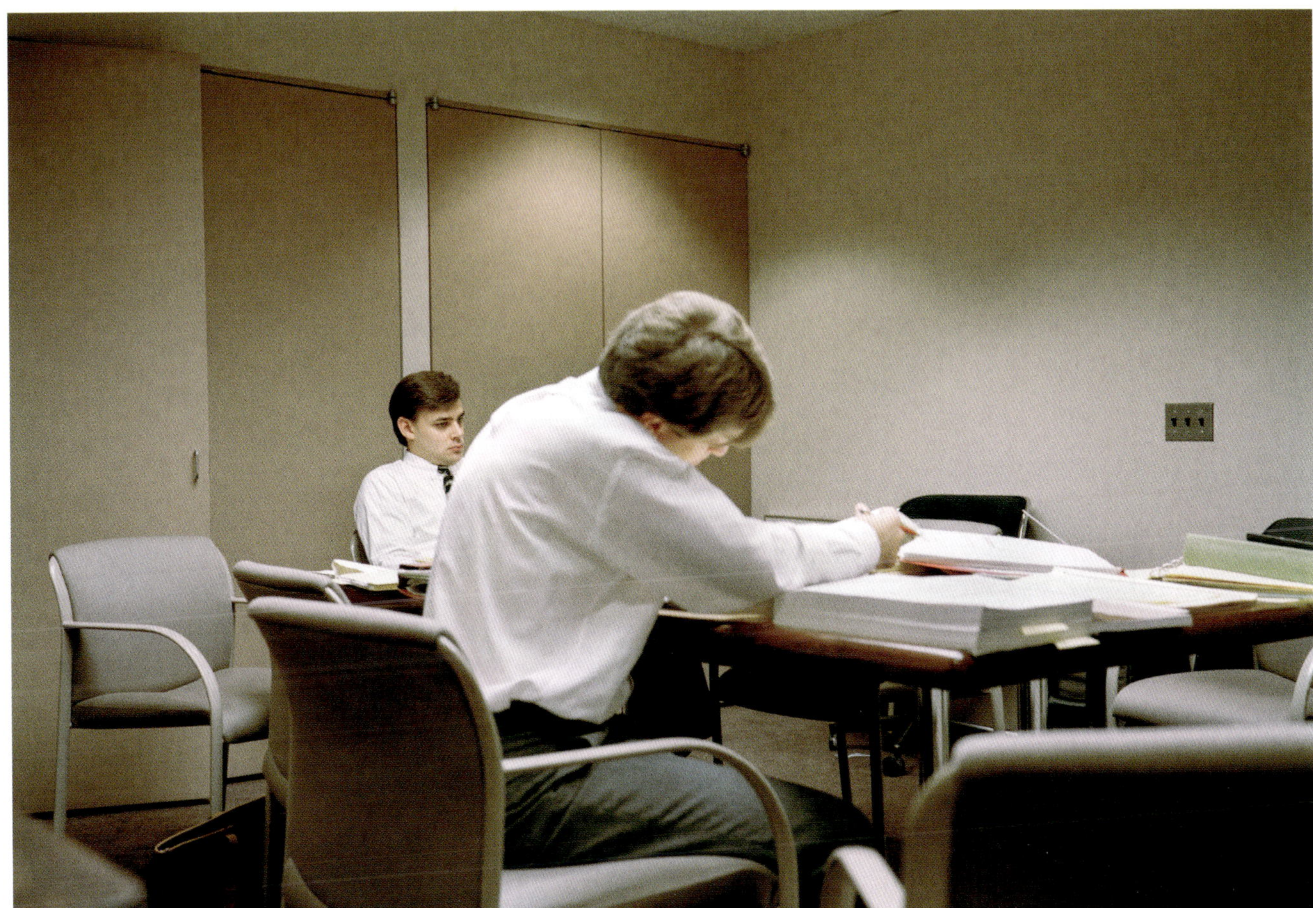

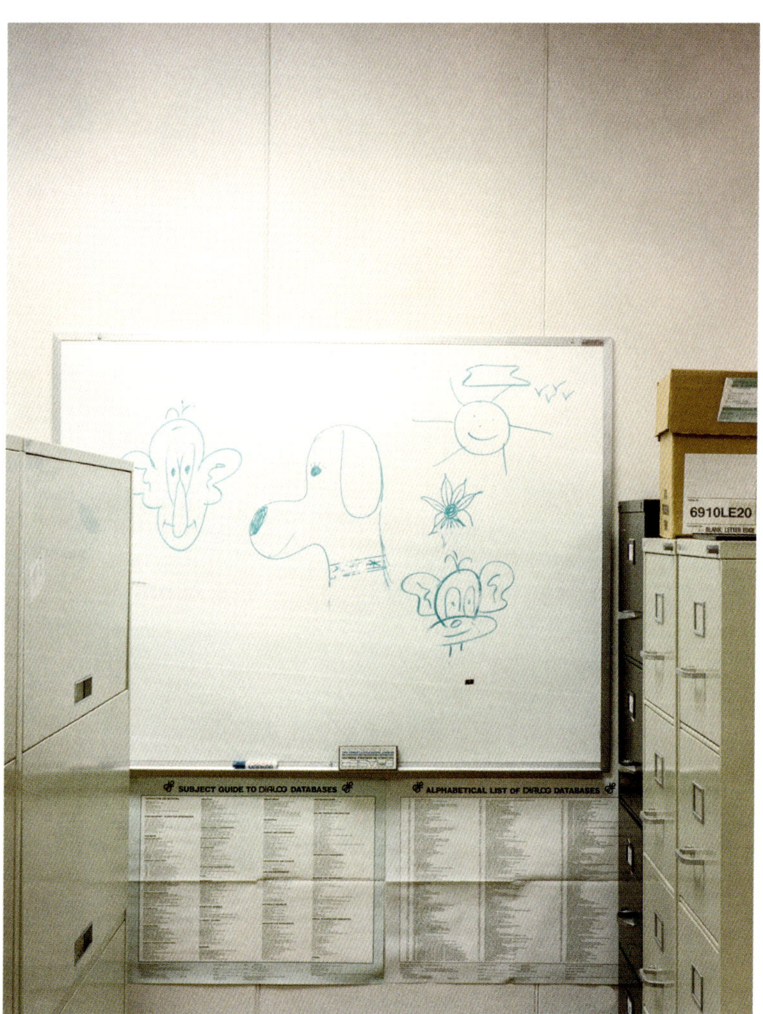

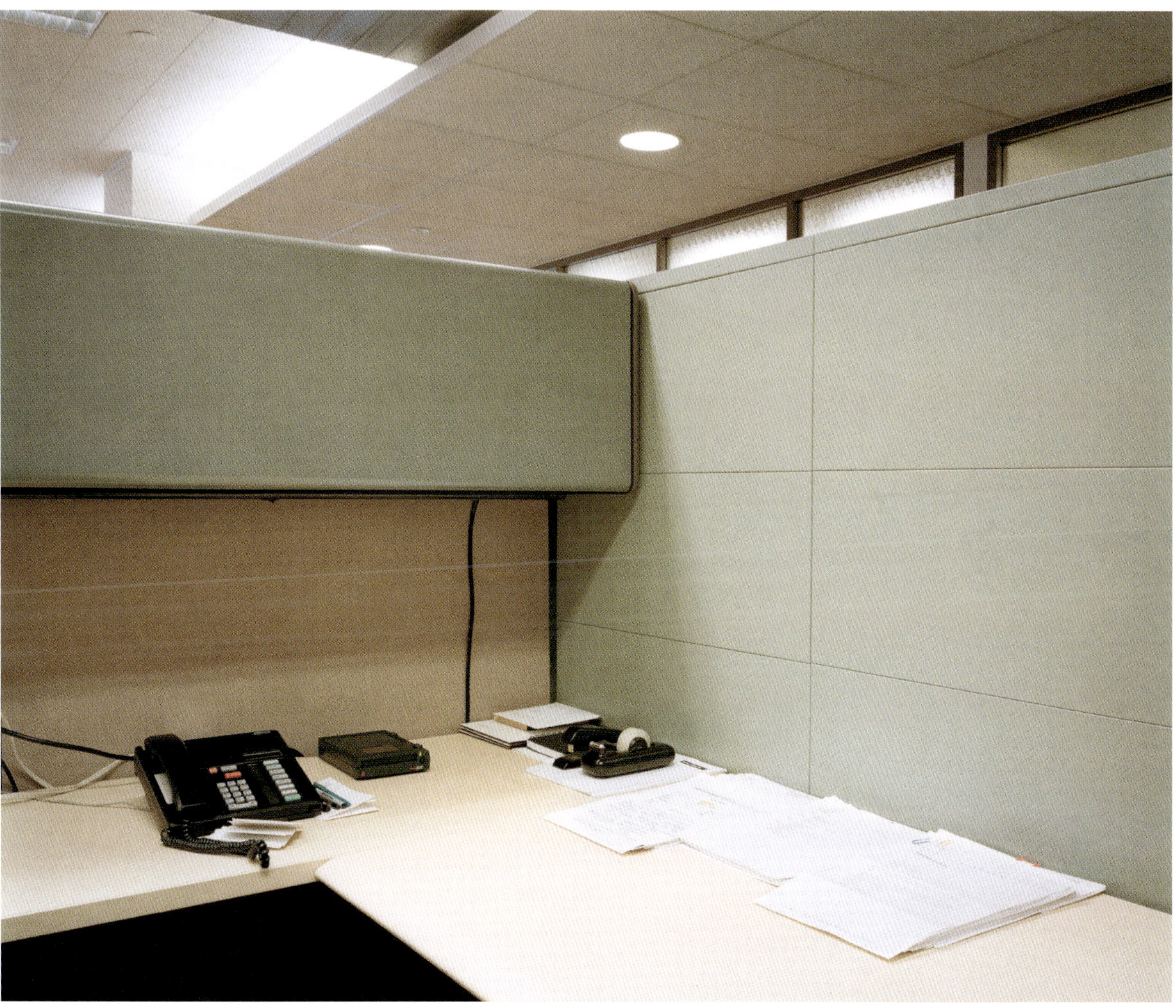

Commercial Bank

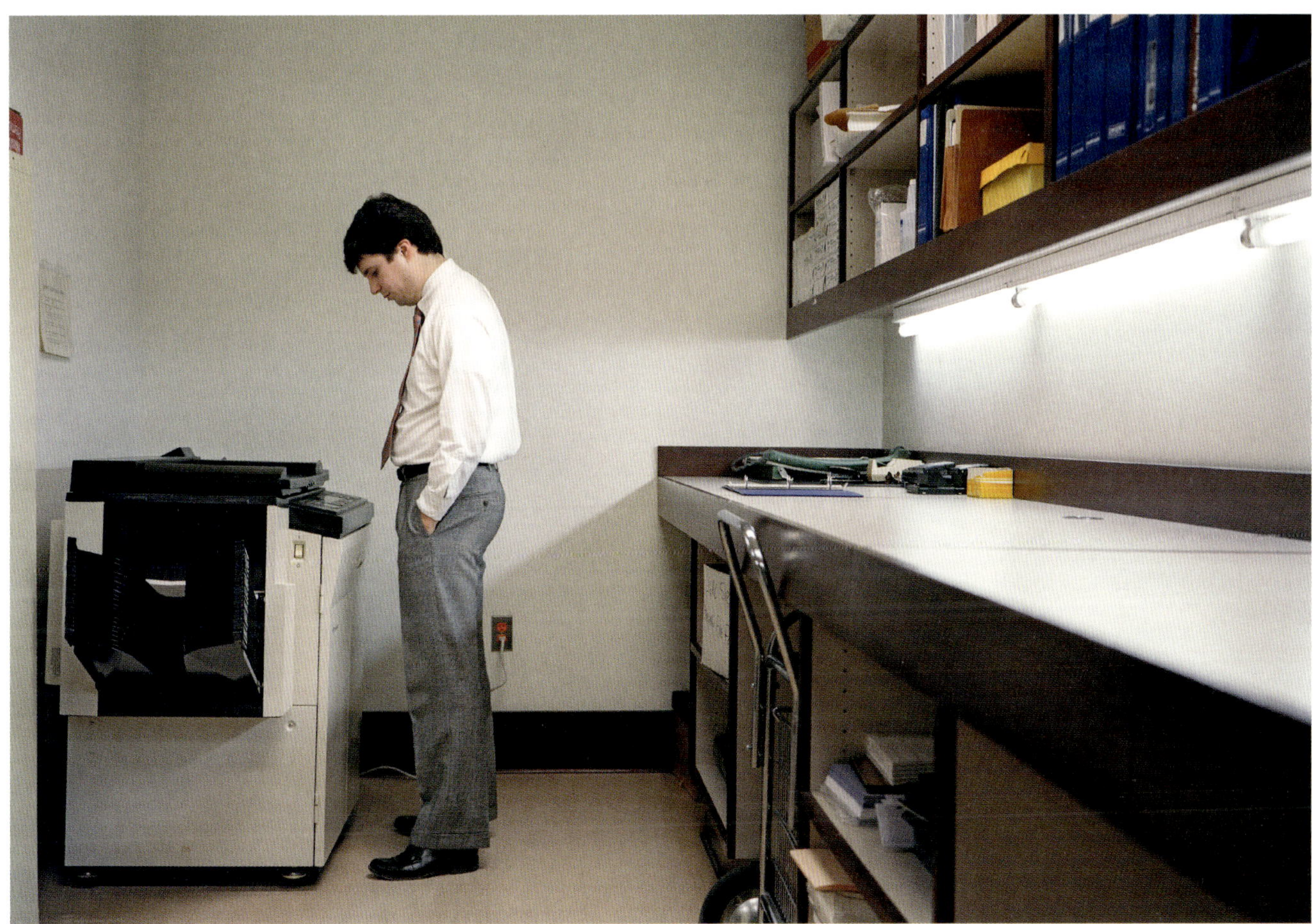

Savings and Loan Company

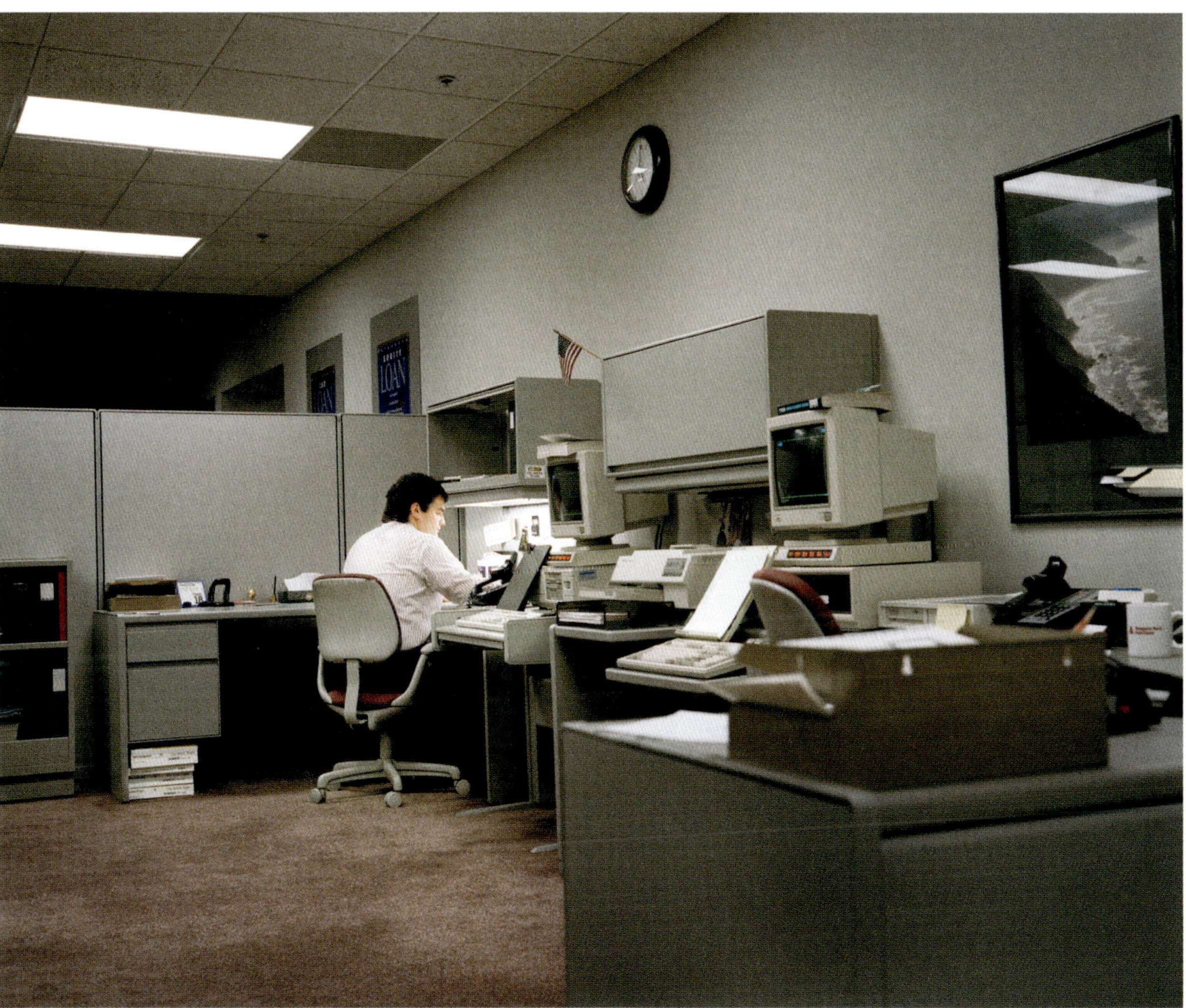

Public Electric Utility

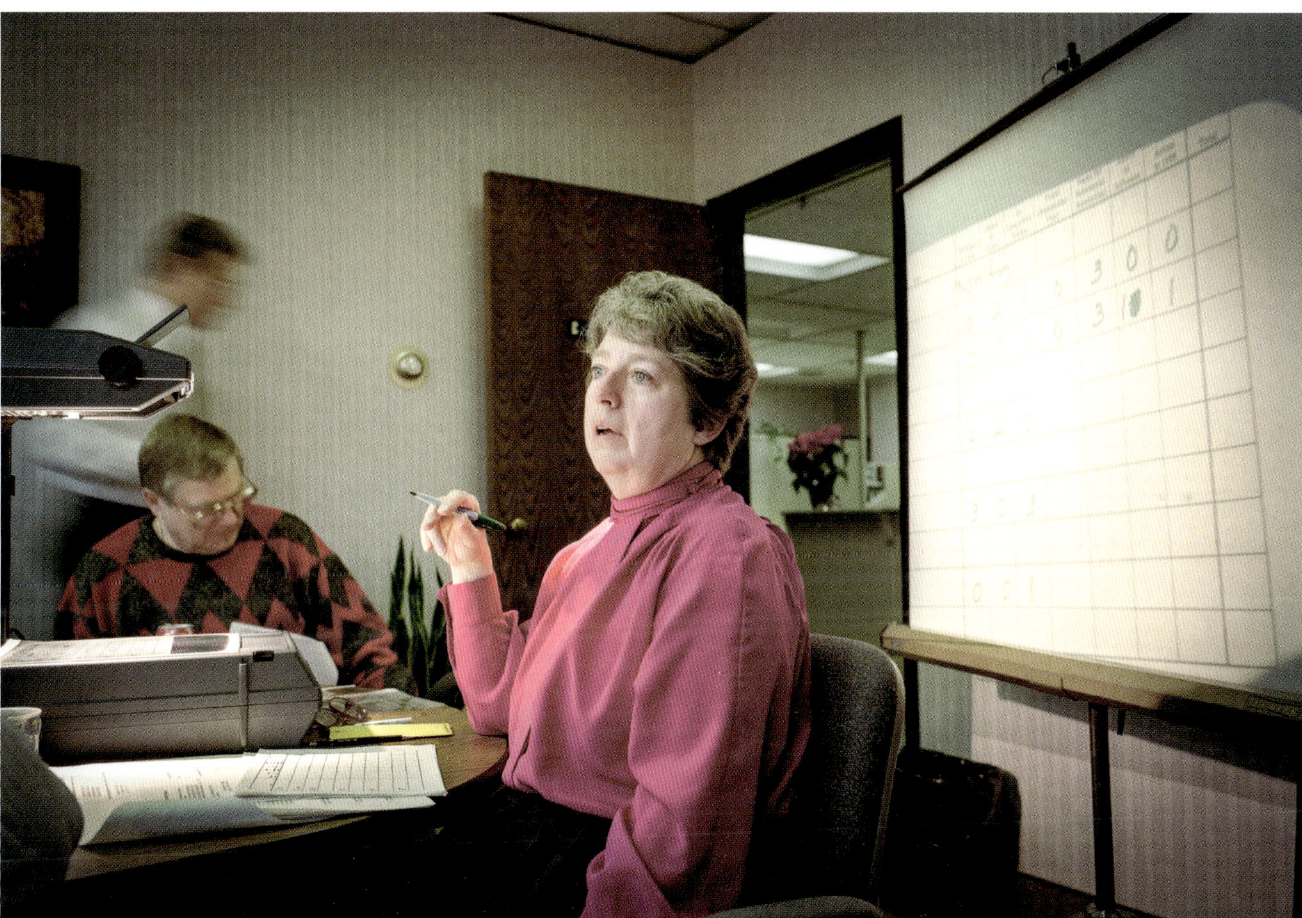

Commercial Bank

overleaf: Accounting Firm *(left),* Government Office *(right)*

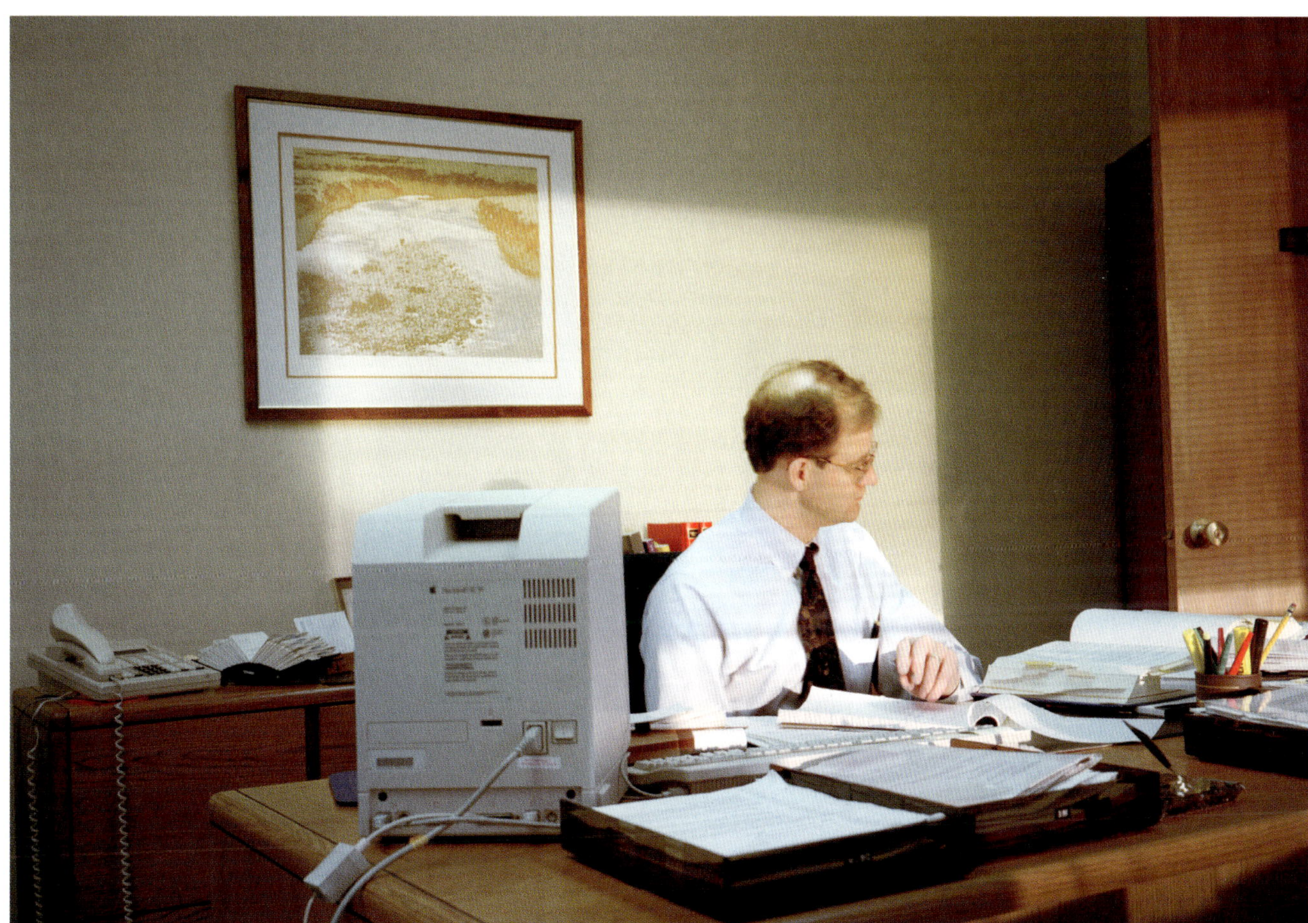

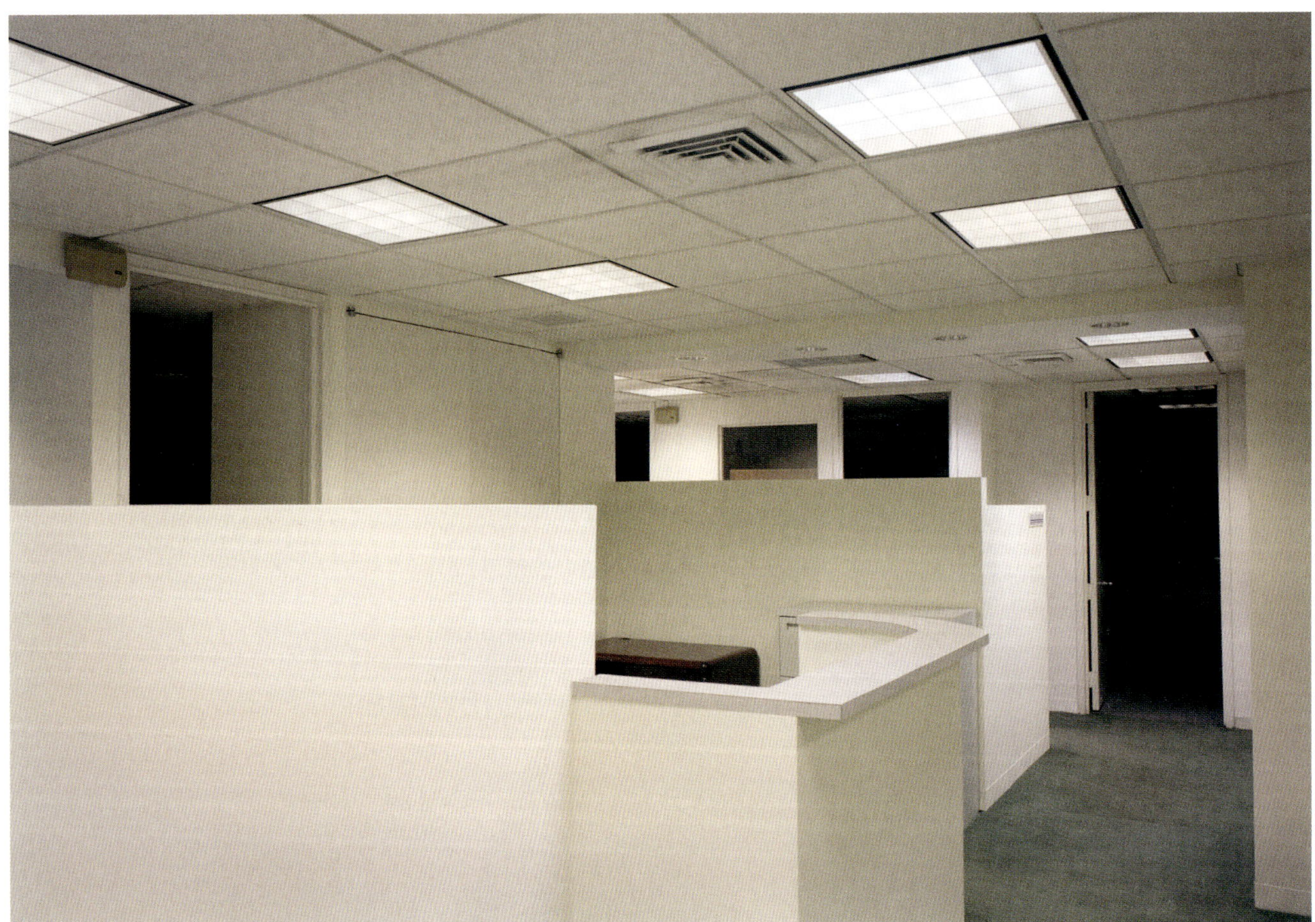

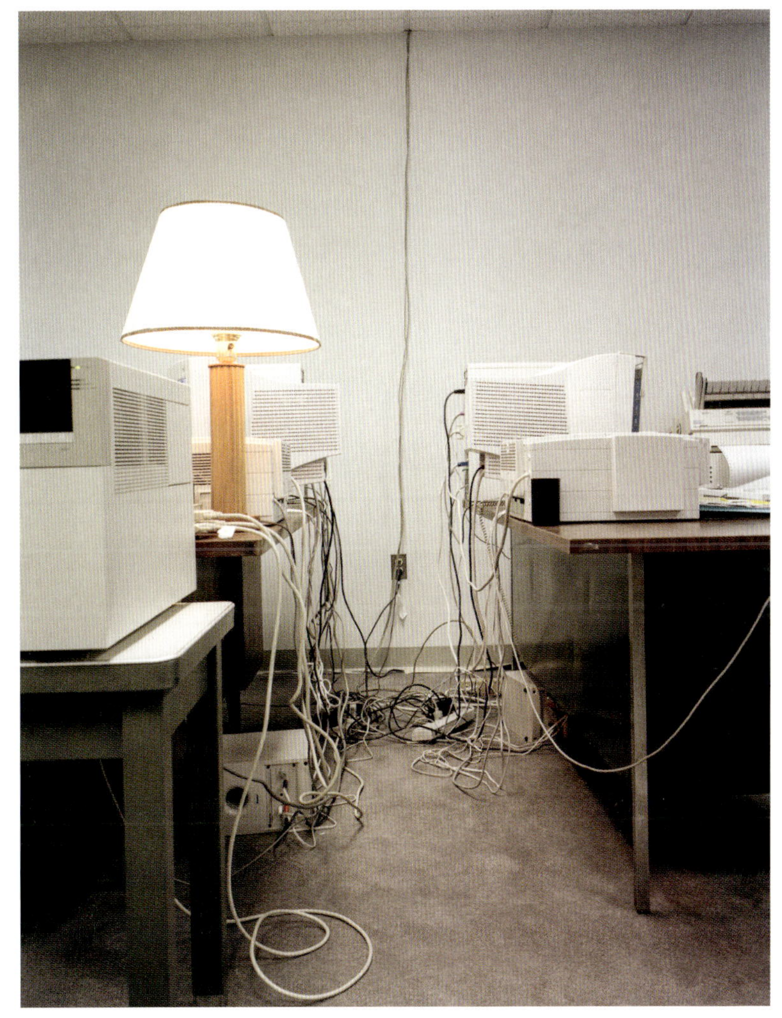

Commercial Bank

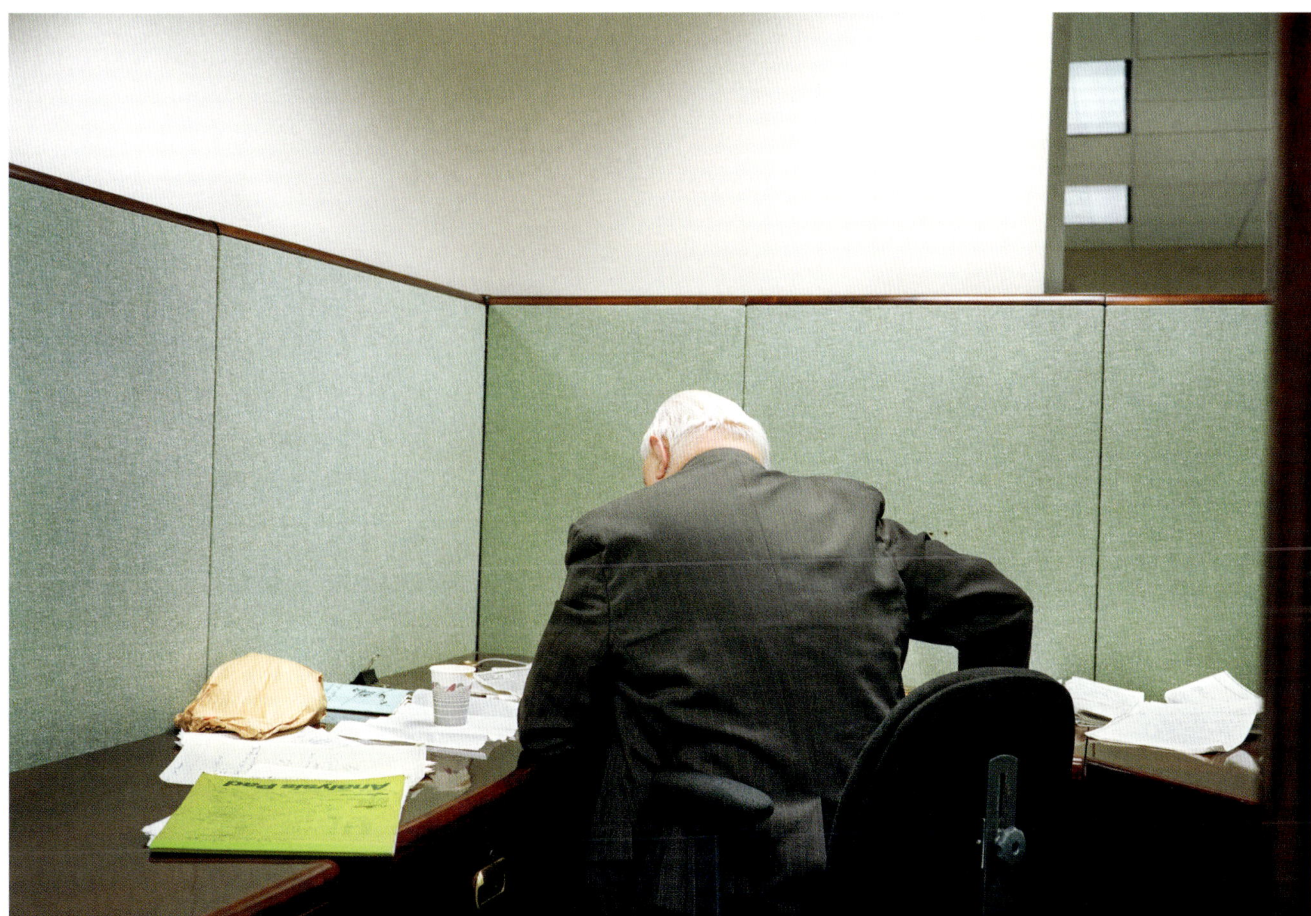
Analysis pad

Office Technology Company

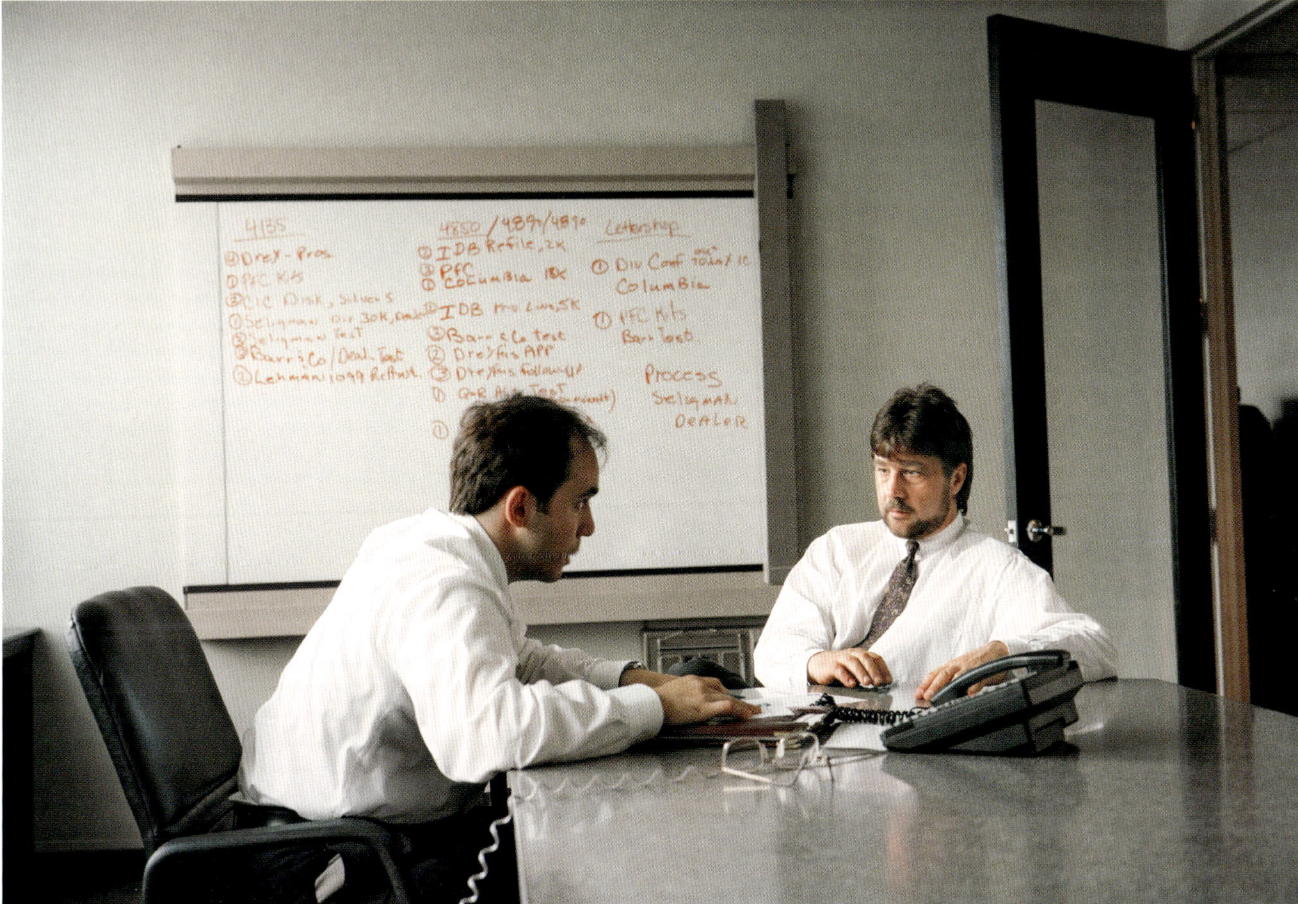

Accounting Firm

overleaf: Government Office

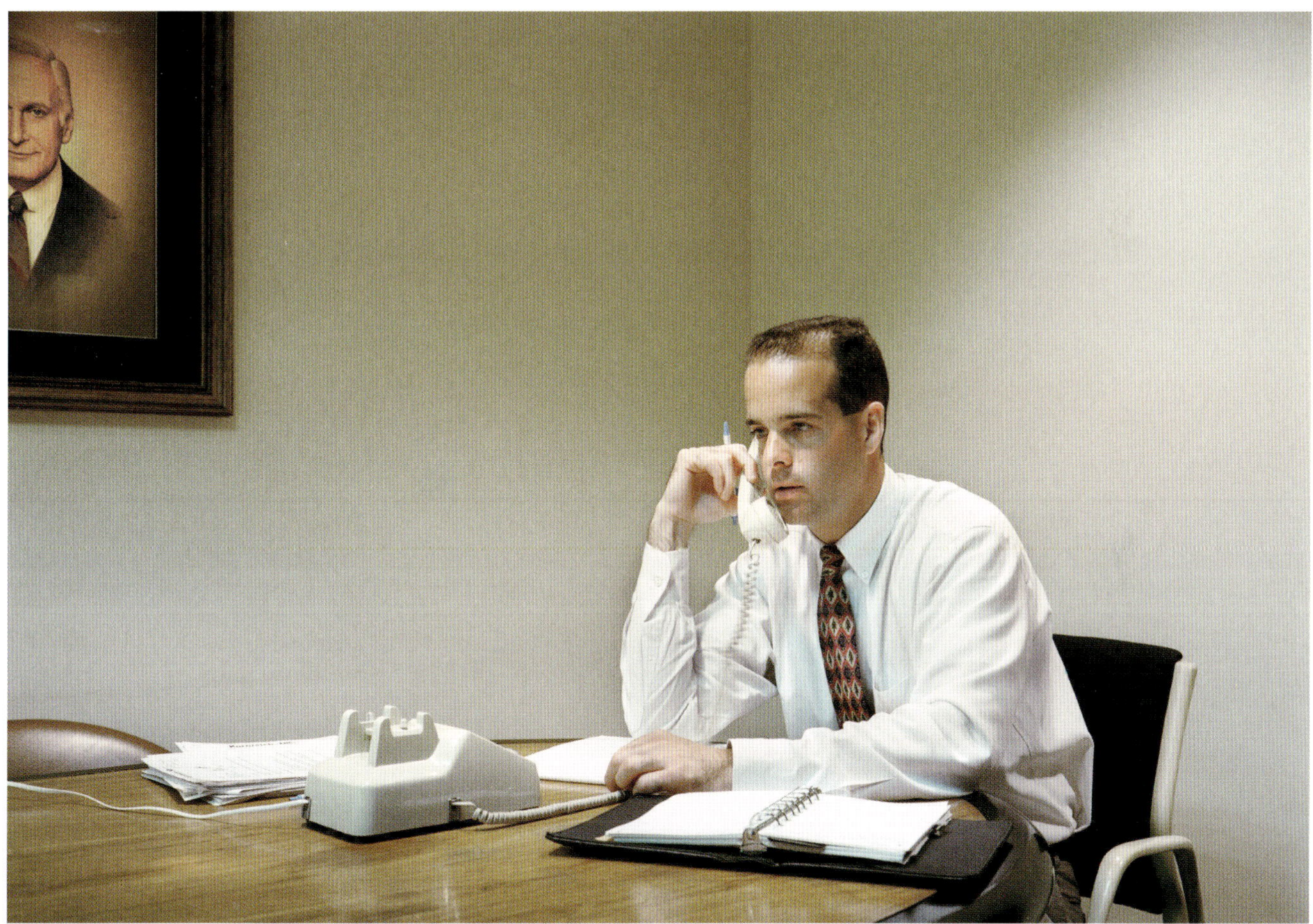

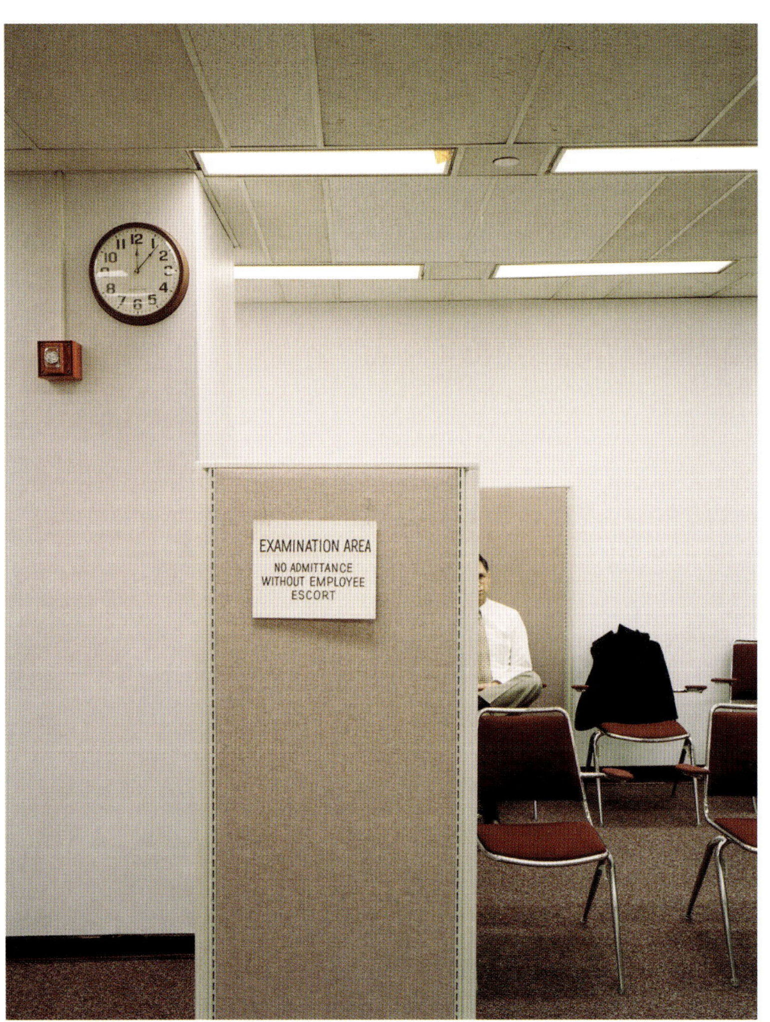
EXAMINATION AREA
NO ADMITTANCE
WITHOUT EMPLOYEE
ESCORT

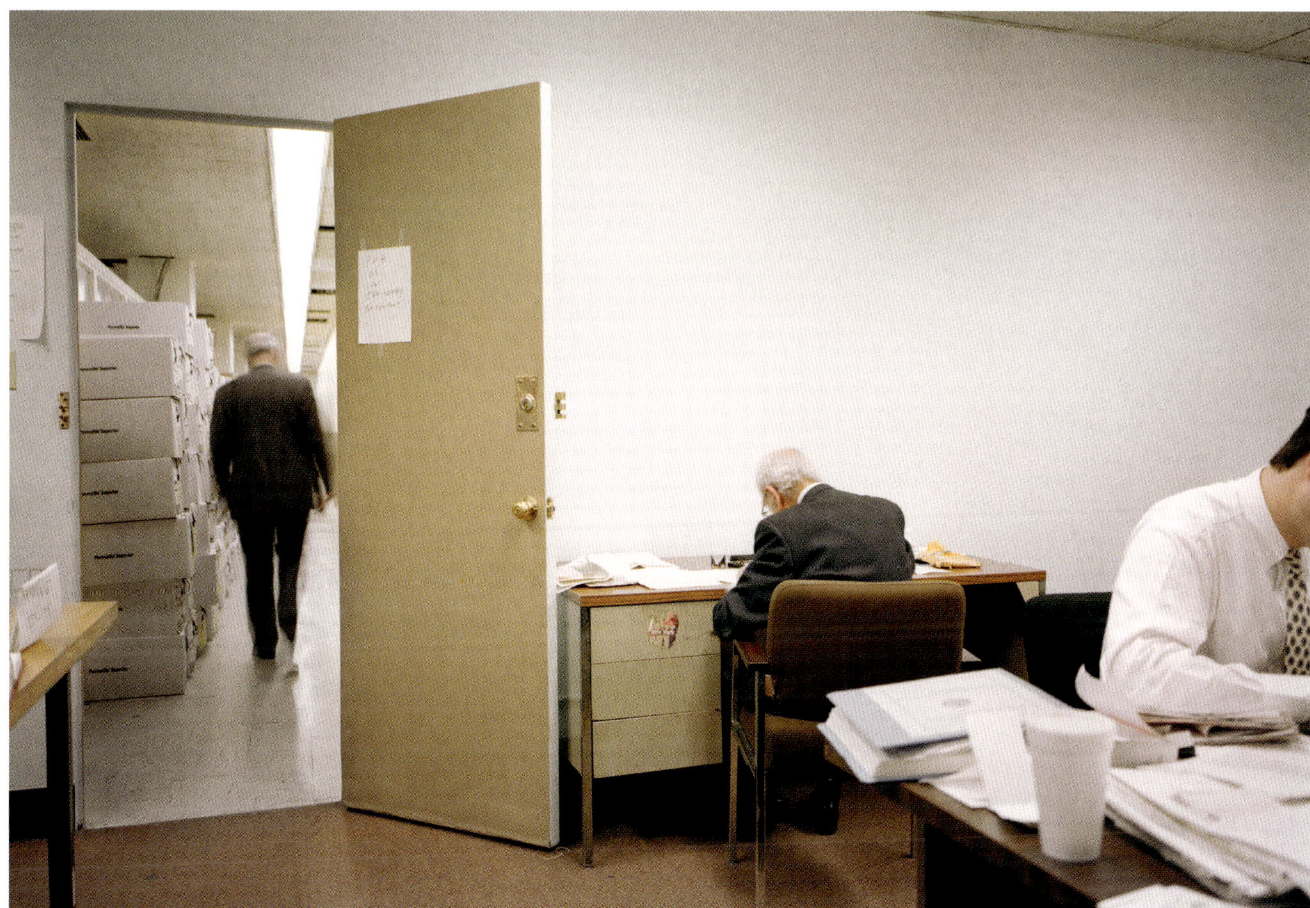

Insurance Company

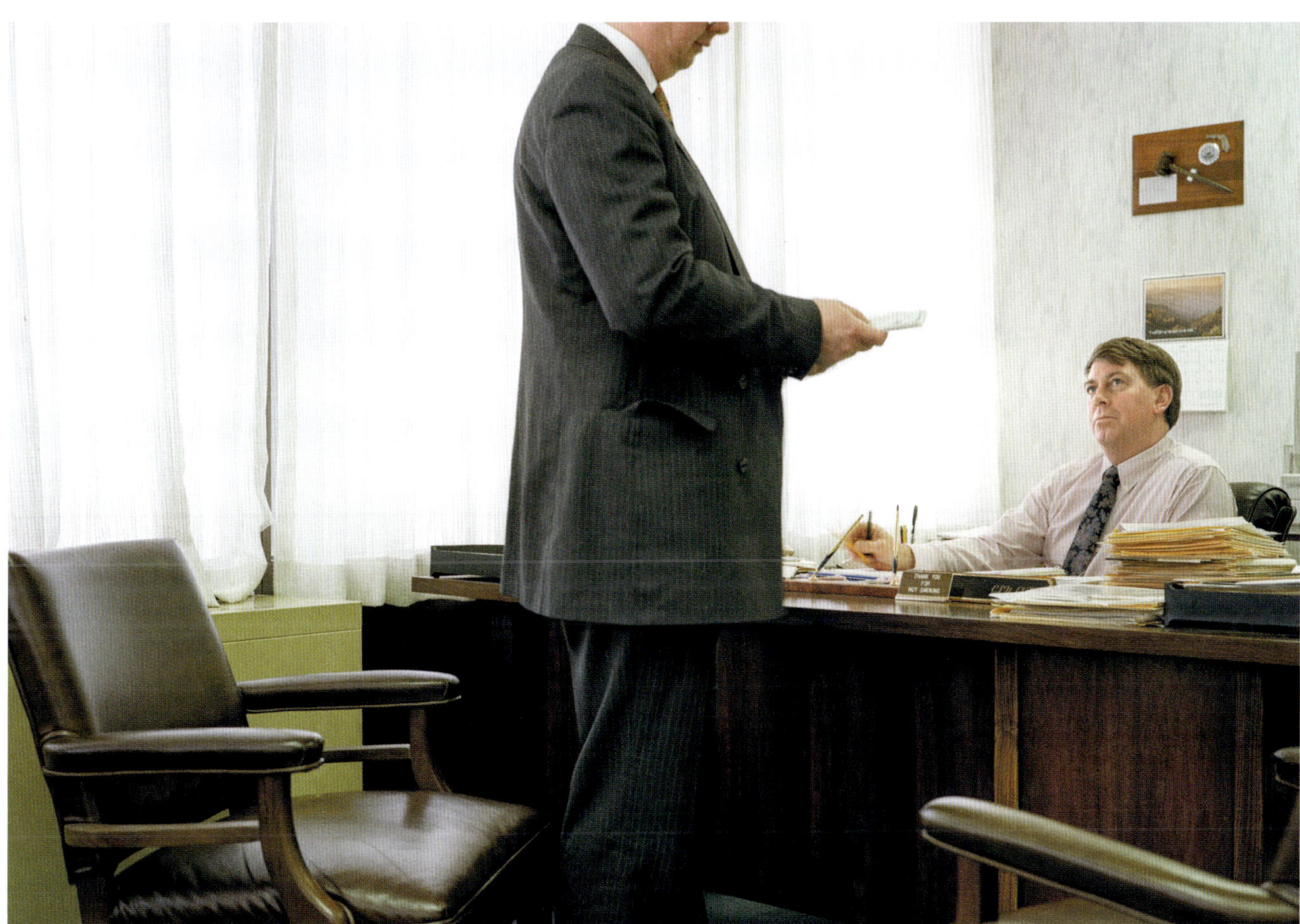

Financial Advisory Firm

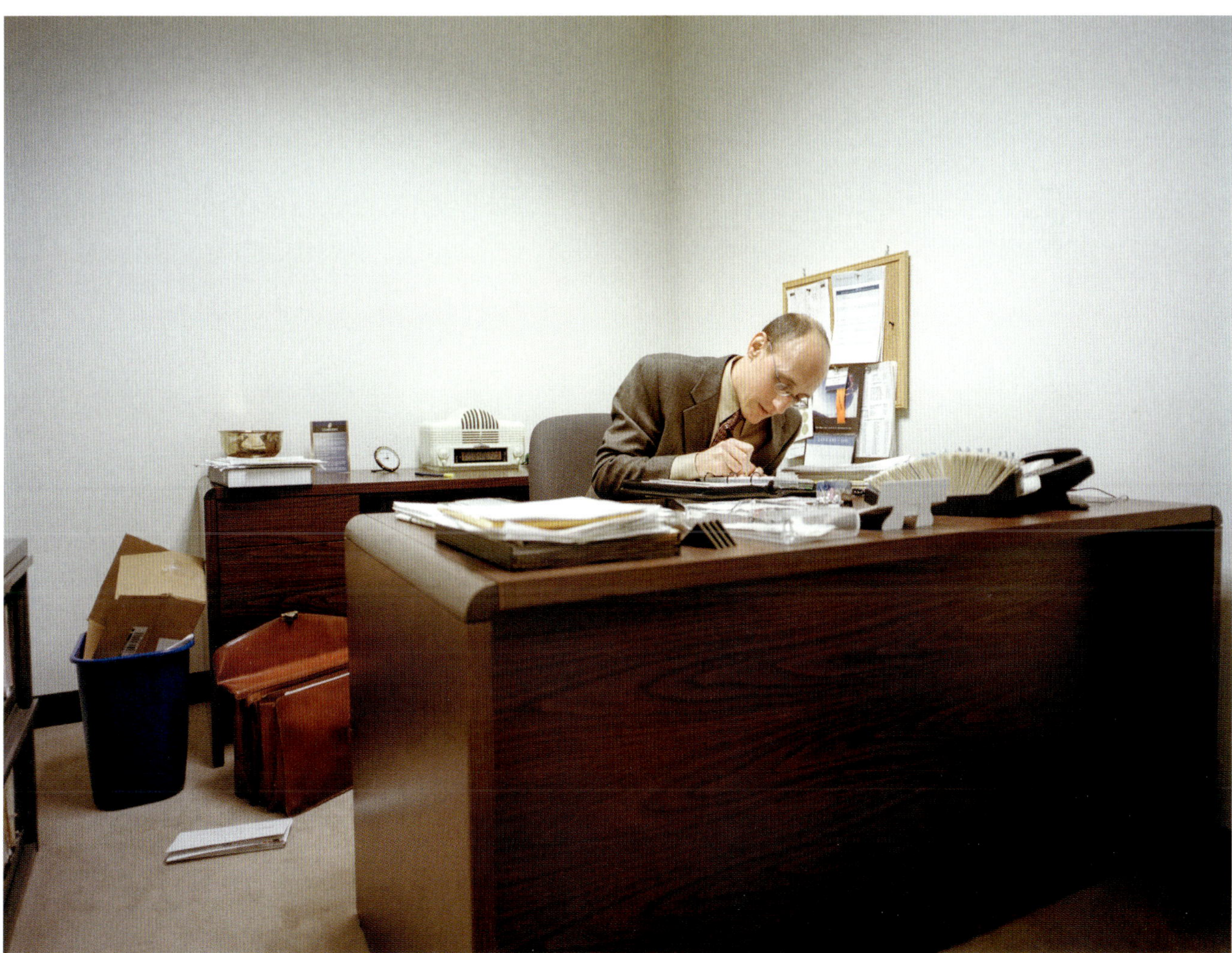

Law Firm

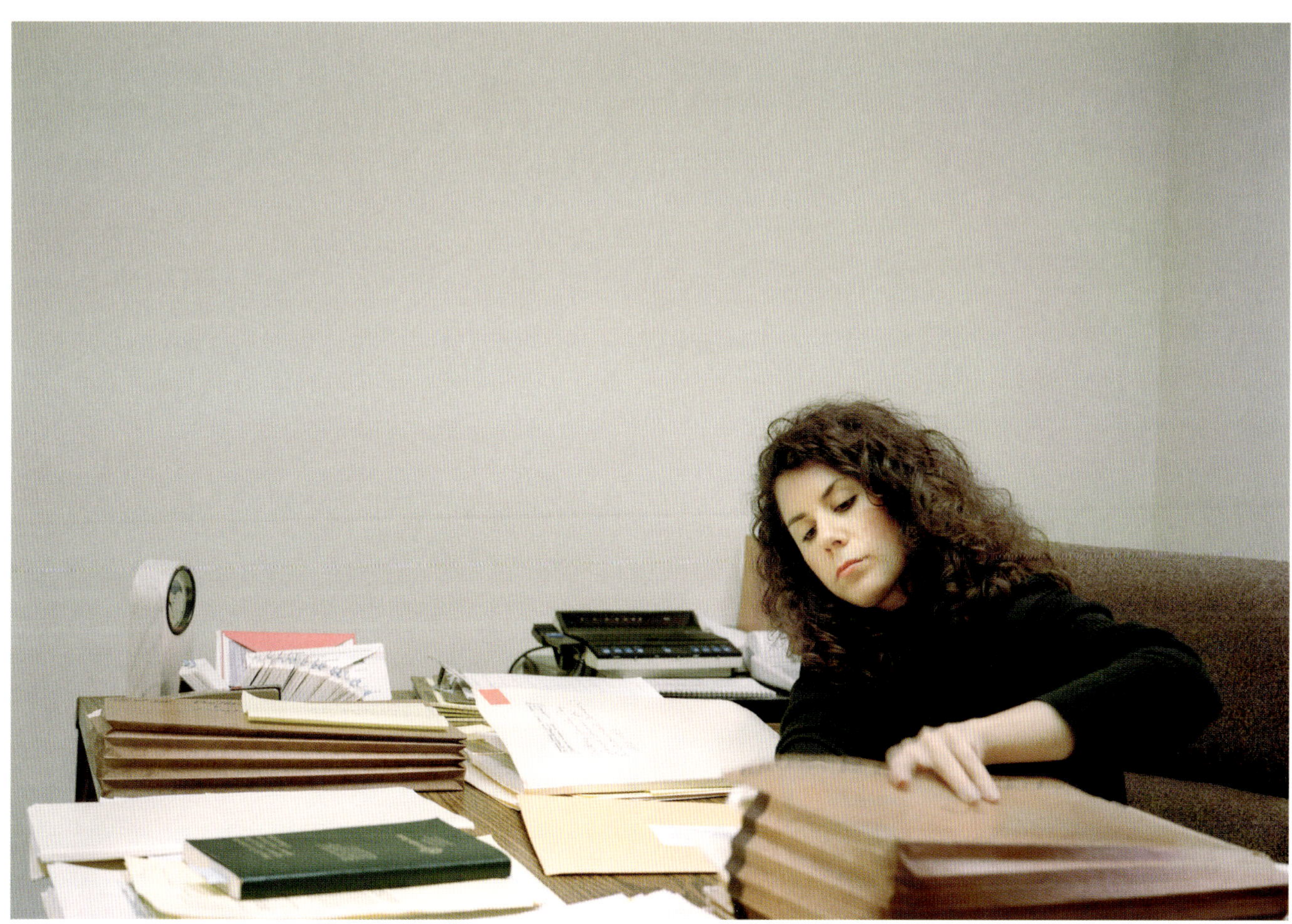

Law Firm

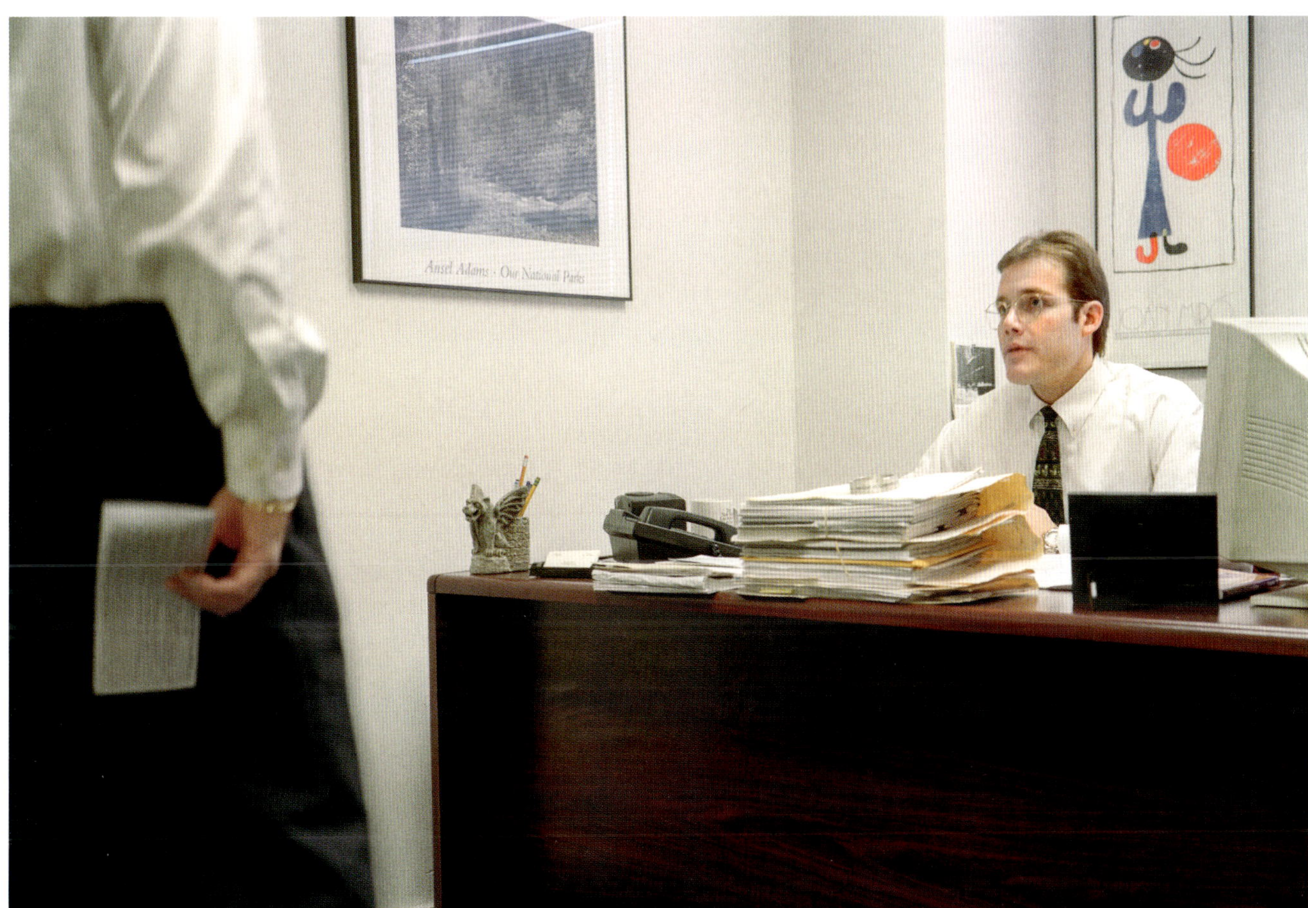

Ansel Adams · Our National Parks

Investment Firm

overleaf: Law Firm *(left)*, Commercial Bank *(right)*

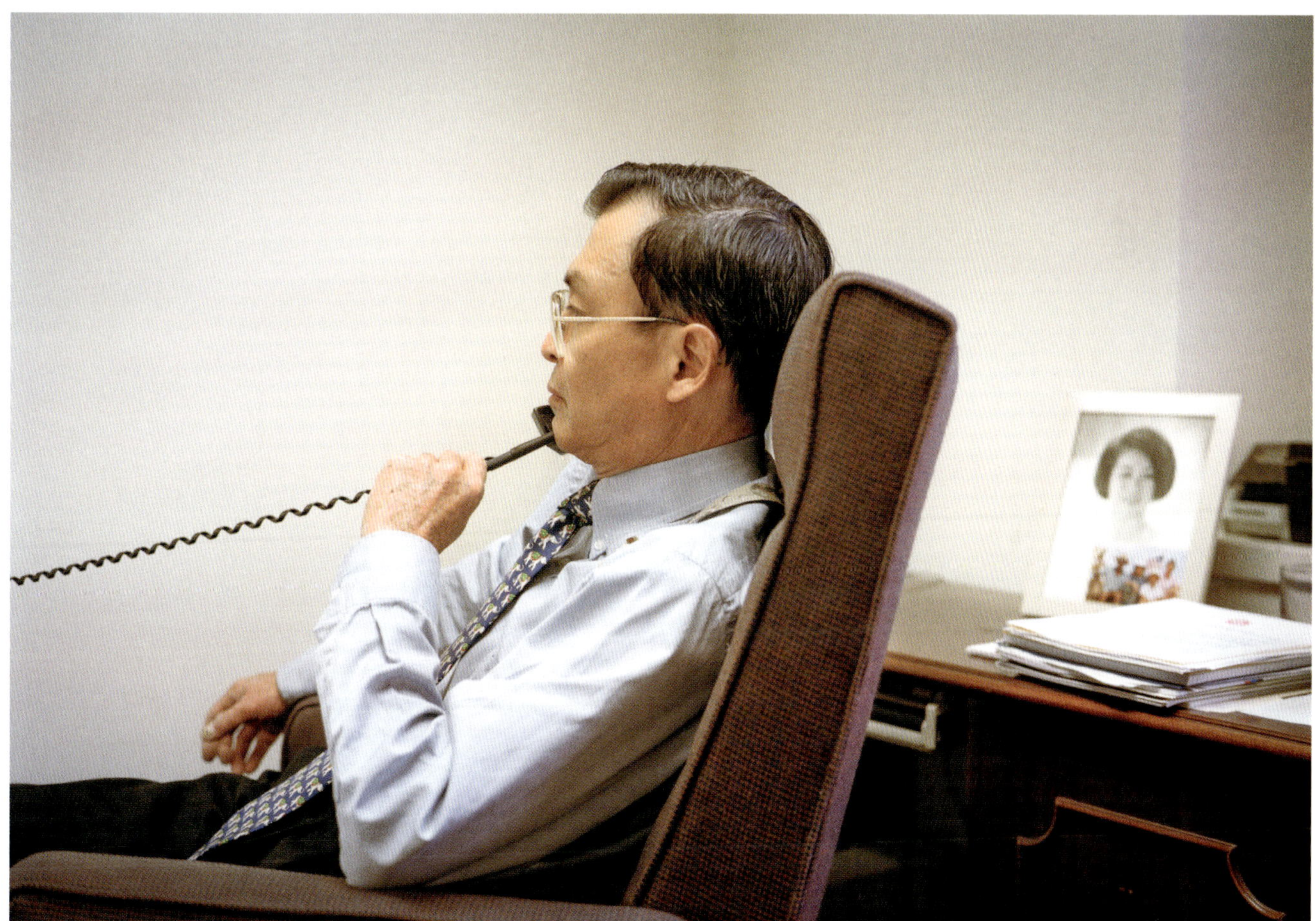

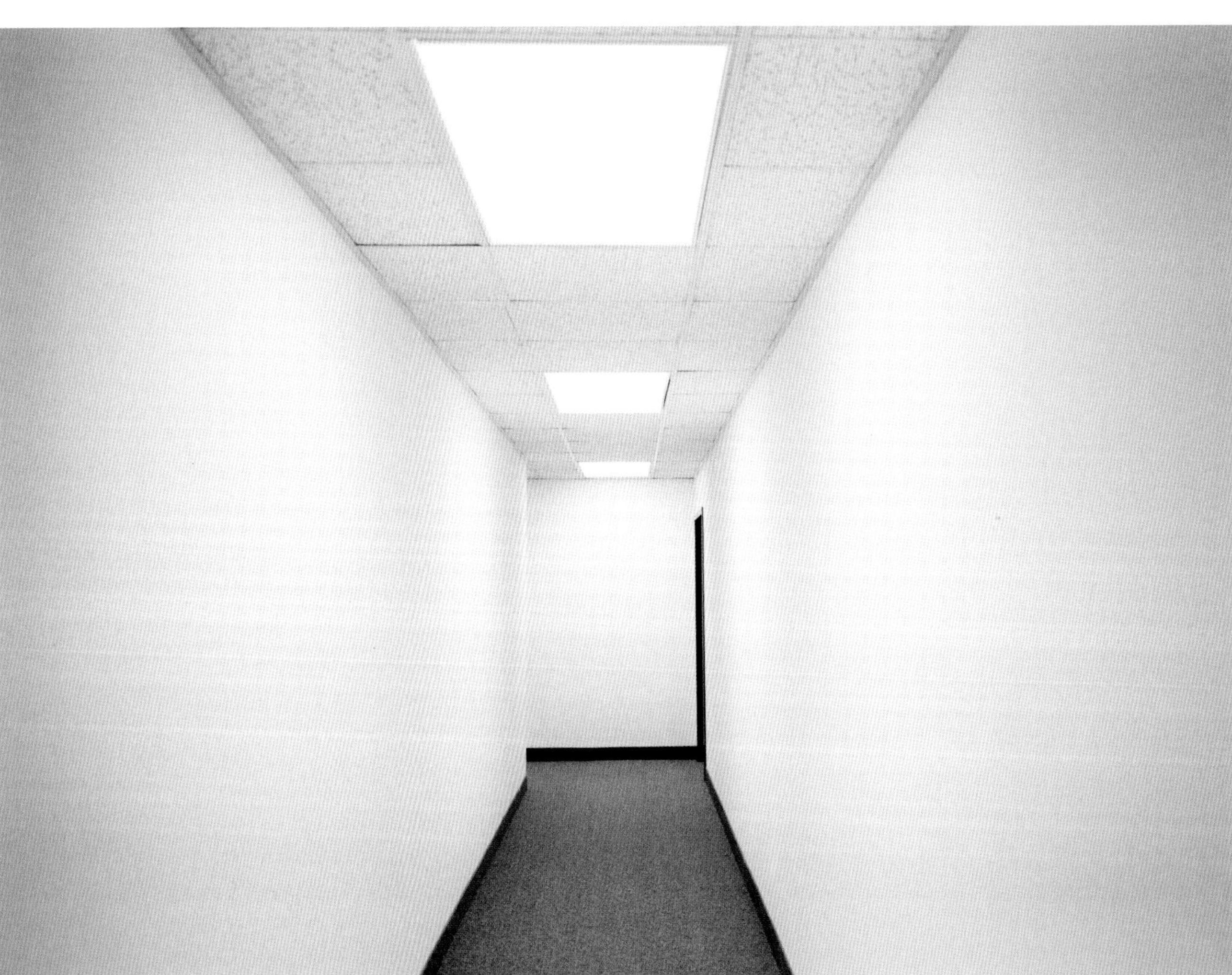

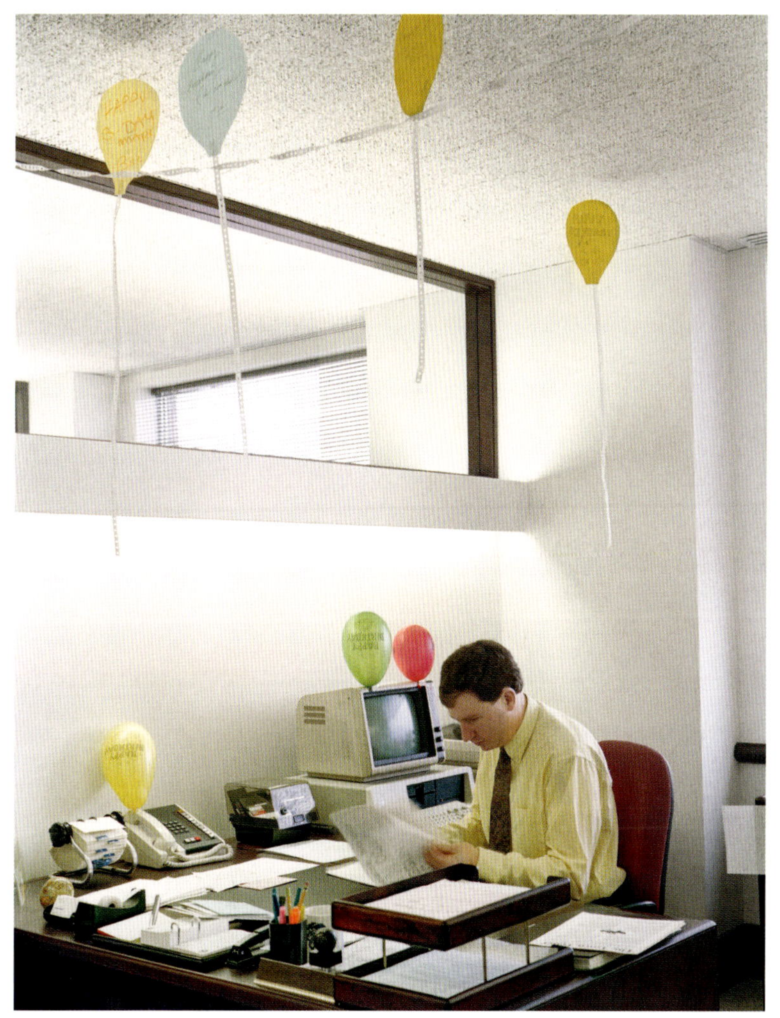

Government Office

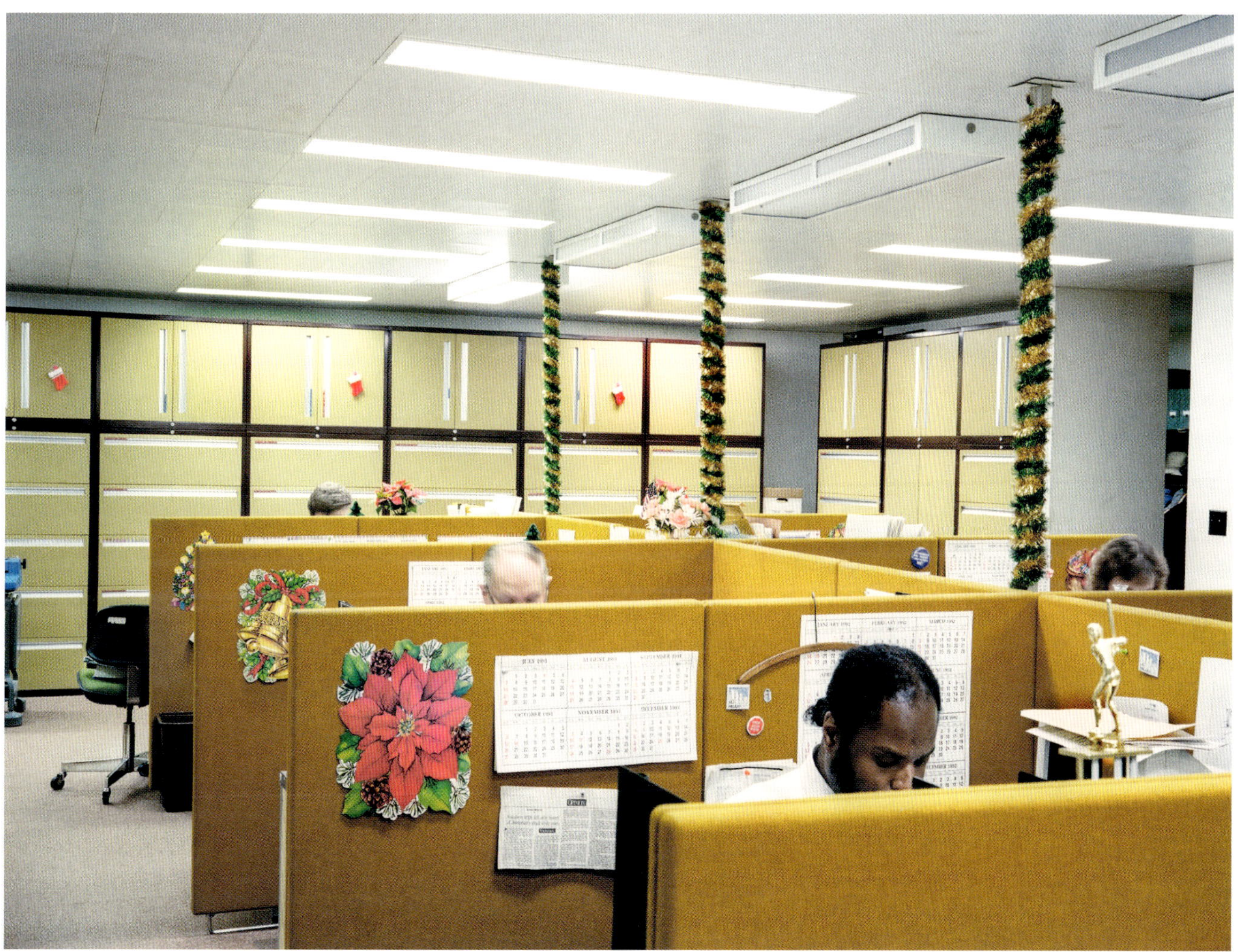

Public Water Utility

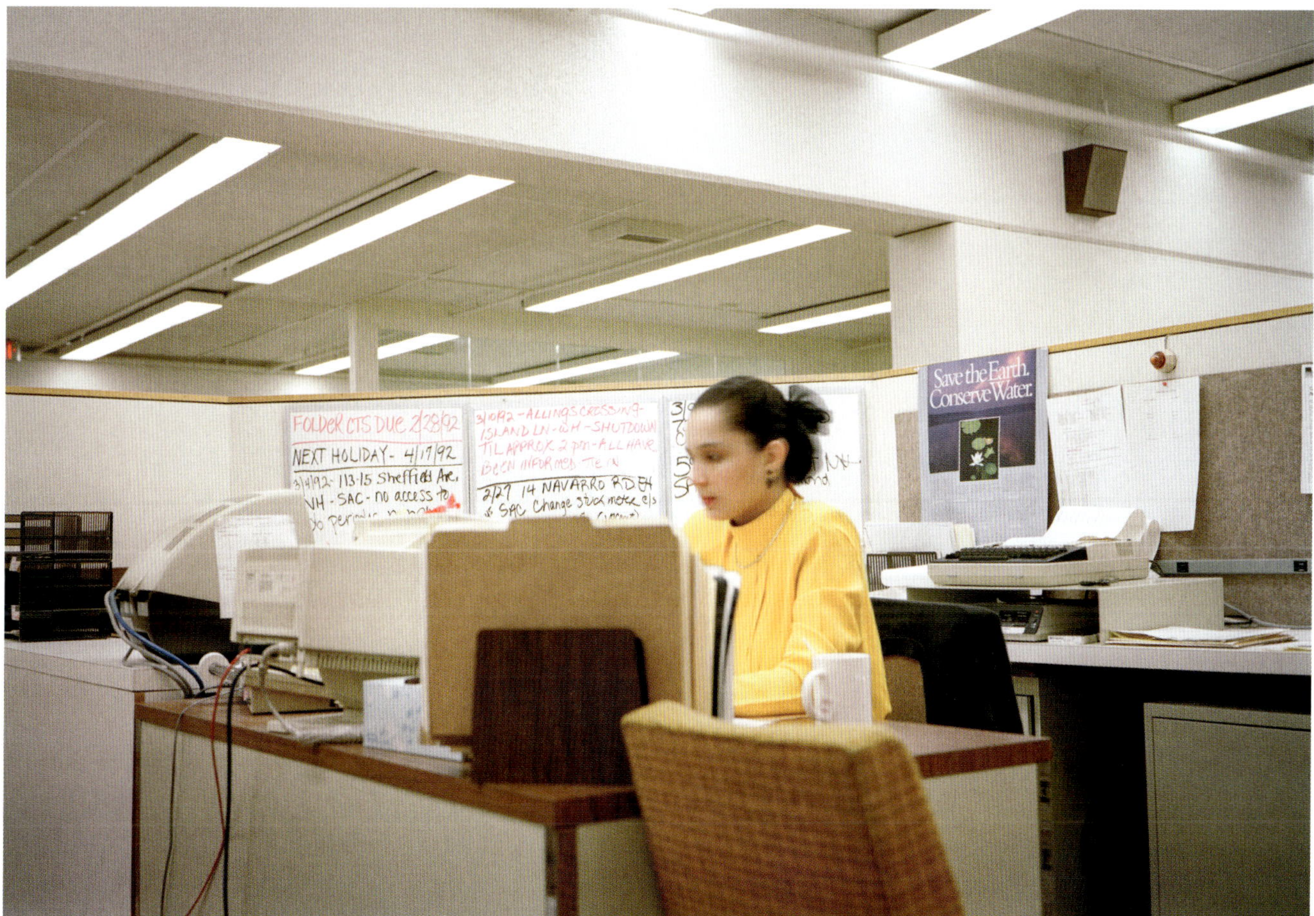
FOLDER CTS DUE 2/28/92
NEXT HOLIDAY - 4/17/92
3/4/92 - 113-15 Sheffield Ave.
VH - SAC - no access to
do permit in no
3/10/92 - ALLINGS CROSSING -
ISLAND LN - WH - SHUTDOWN
TIL APPROX 2 PM - ALL HAVE
BEEN INFORMED - TE IN
2/27 14 NAVARRO RD E4
SAC change stck meter c/s
Save the Earth.
Conserve Water.

Commercial Bank

overleaf: Accounting Firm *(left),* Office Furniture Manufacturer *(right)*

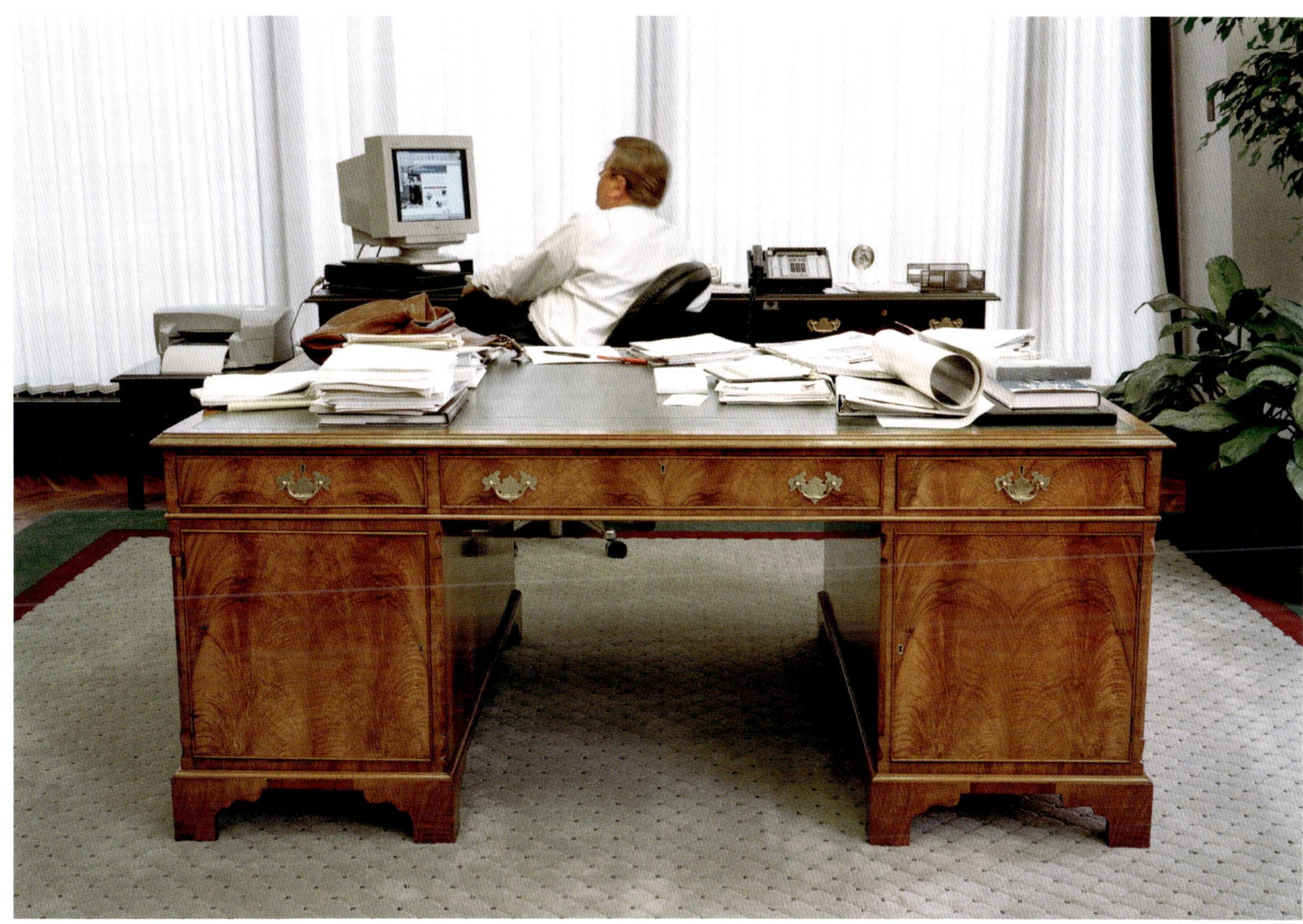

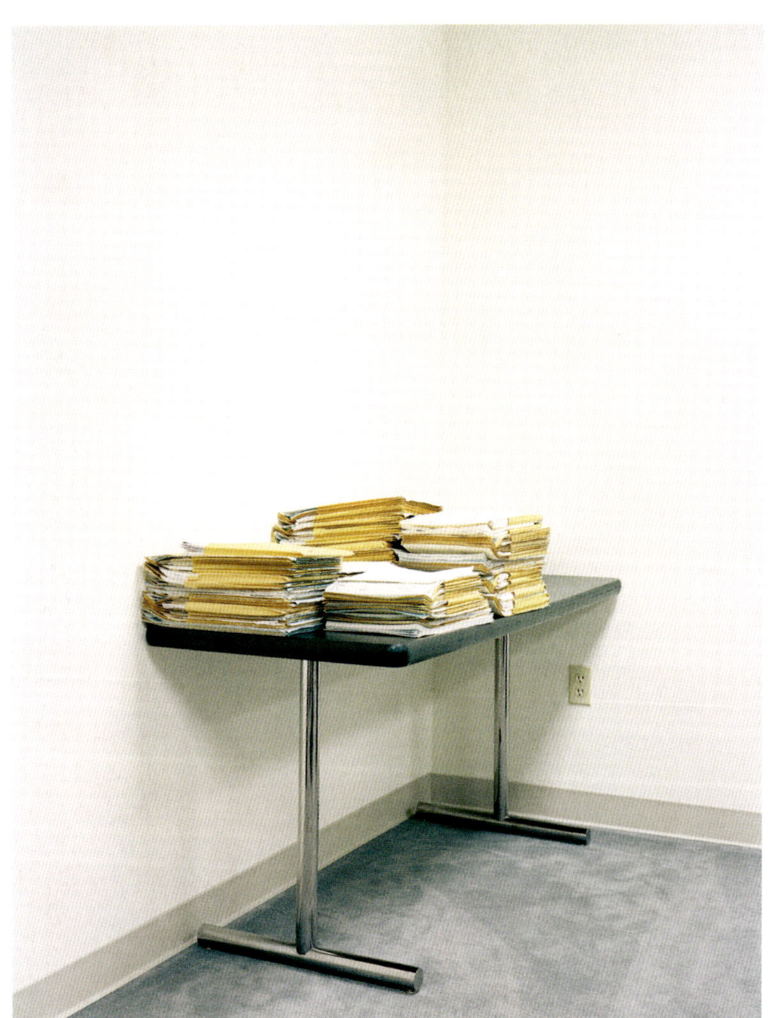

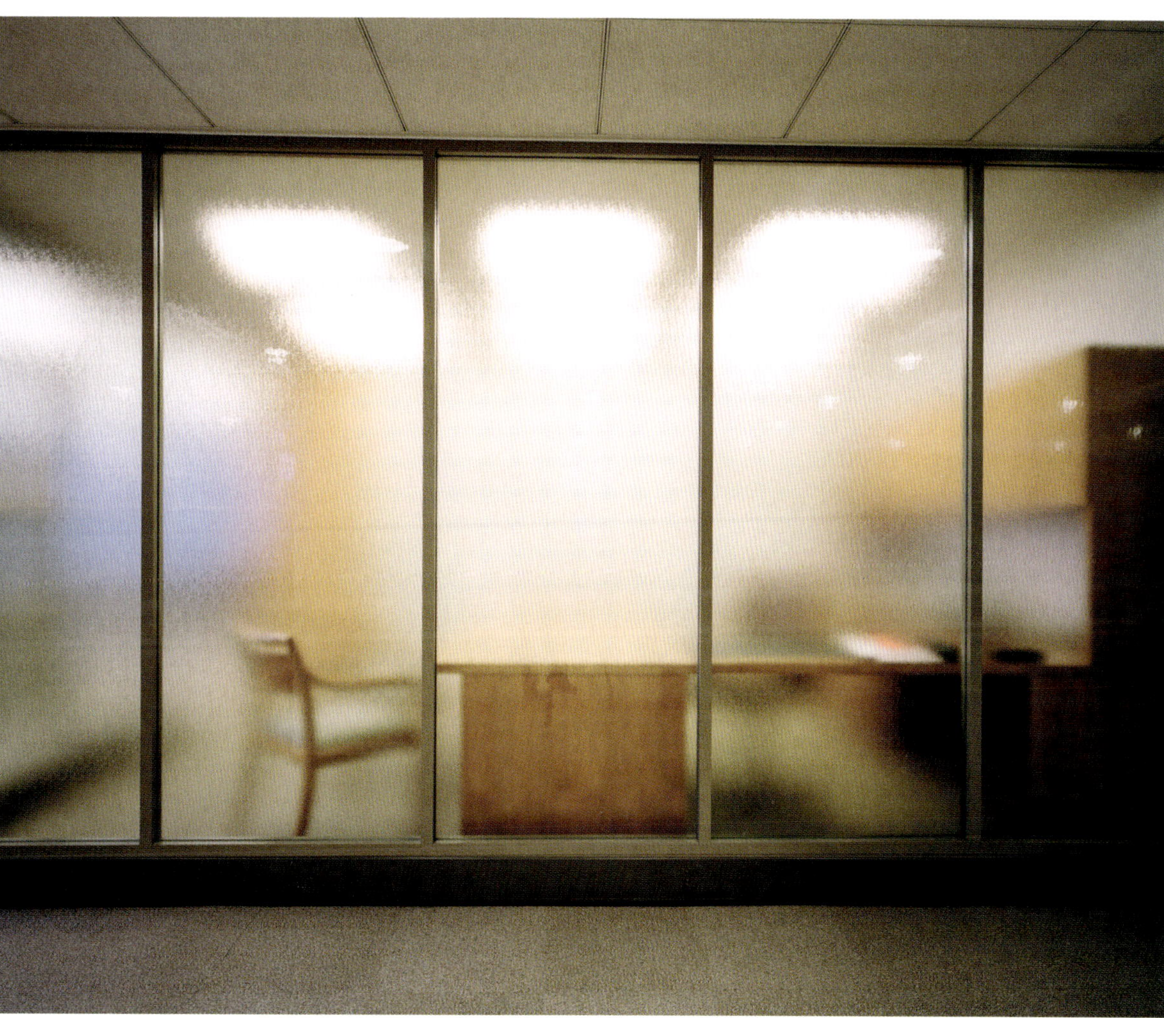

Law Firm

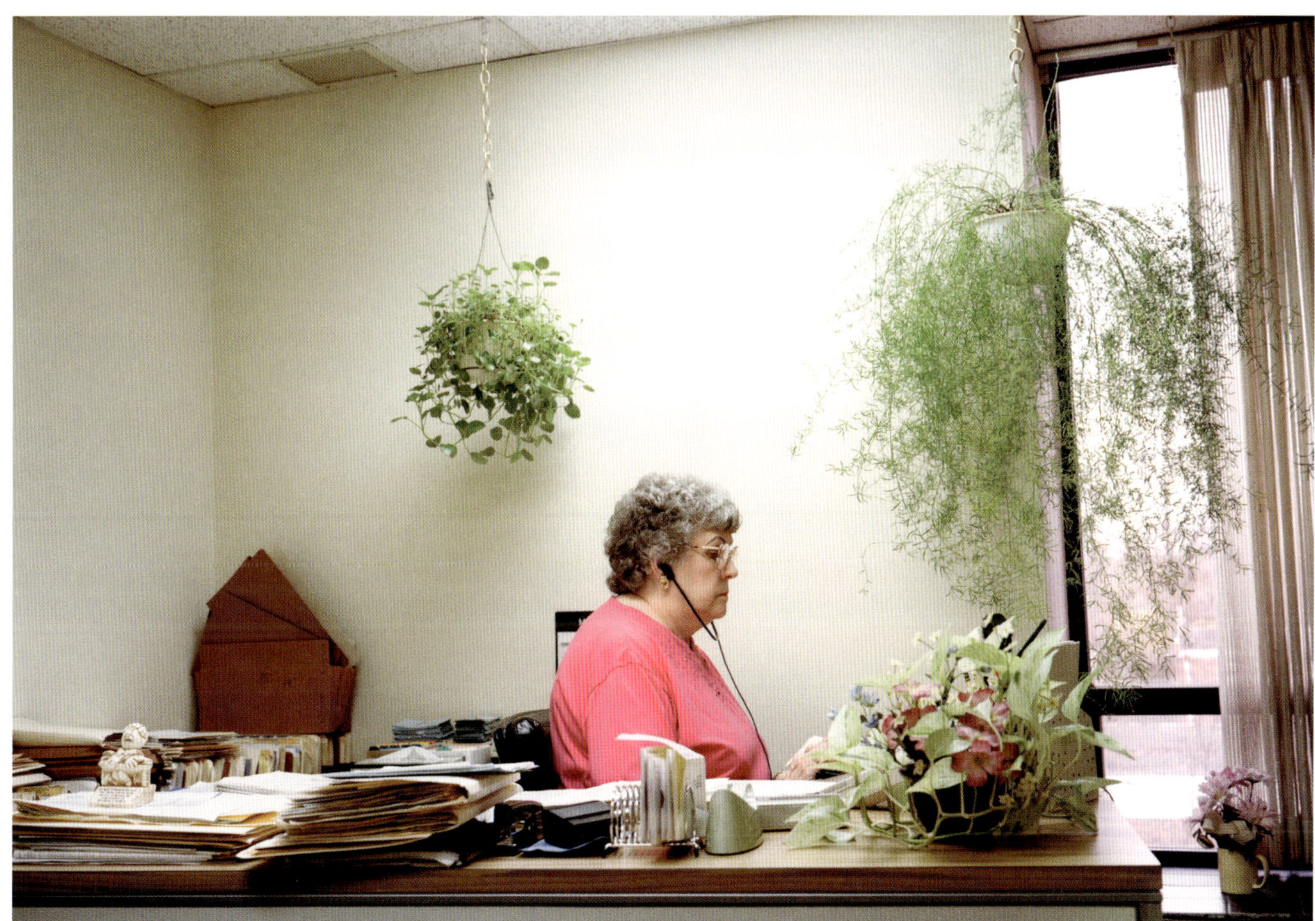

Home Security Company

overleaf: Insurance Company *(left),* Public Electric Utility *(right)*

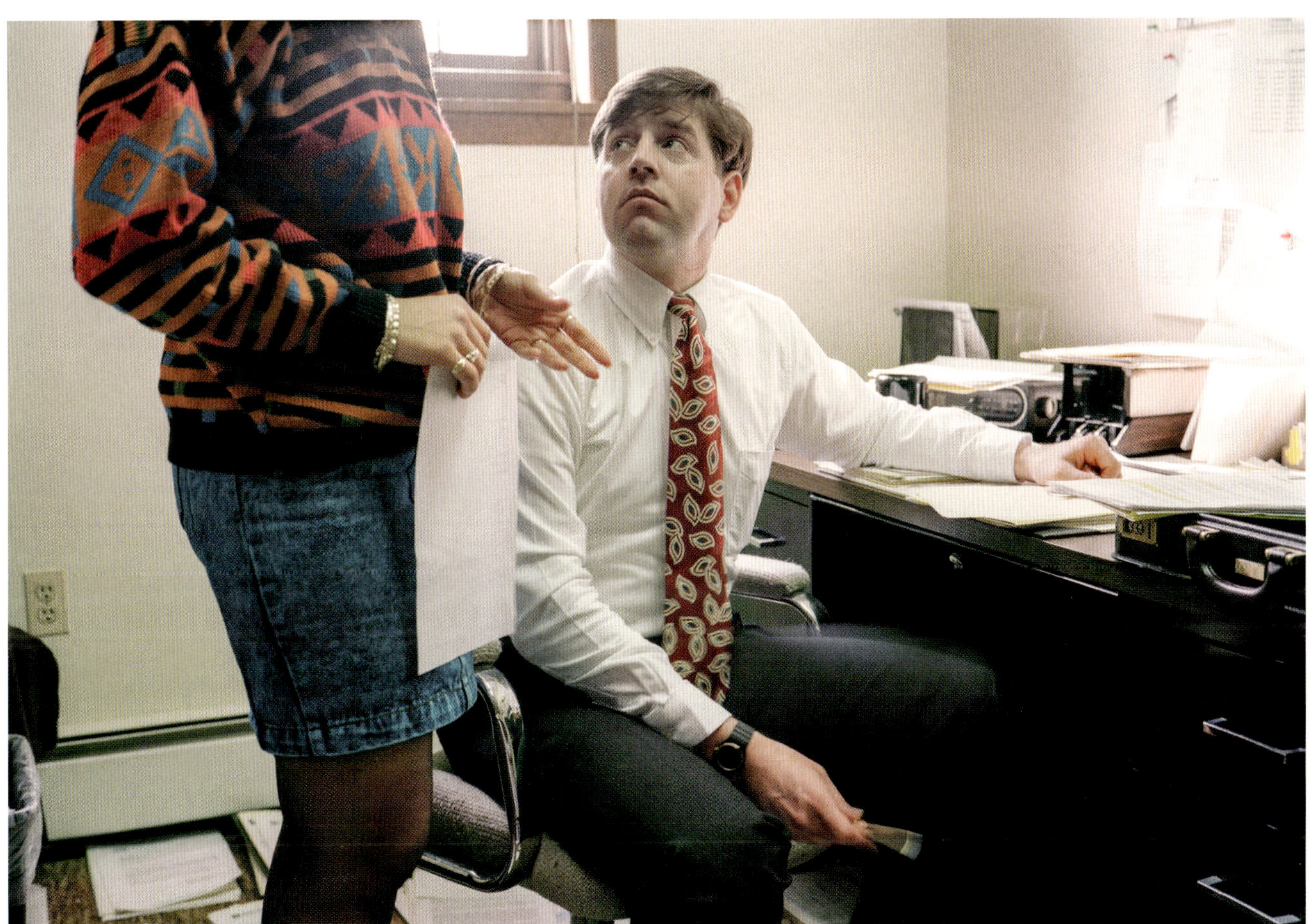

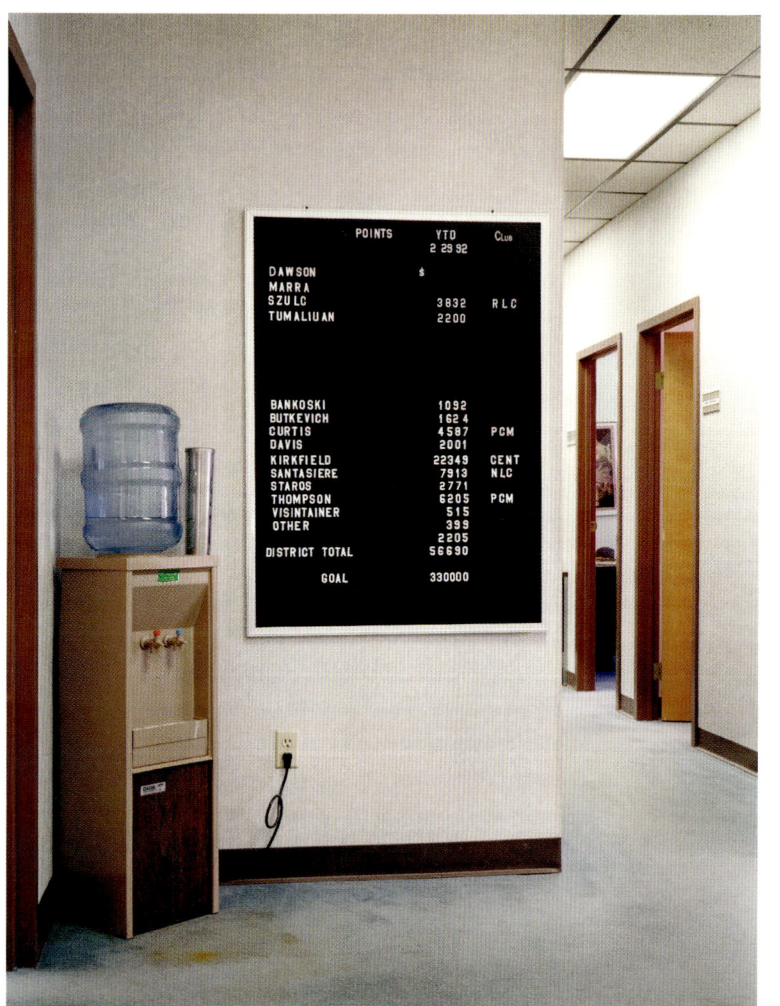

POINTS   YTD   CLUB
              2 29 92
DAWSON $
MARRA
SZULC   3832   RLC
TUMALIUAN   2200

BANKOSKI   1092
BUTKEVICH   162 4
CURTIS   4587   PCM
DAVIS   2001
KIRKFIELD   22349   CENT
SANTASIERE   7913   NLC
STAROS   2771
THOMPSON   6205   PCM
VISINTAINER   515
OTHER   399
                      2205
DISTRICT TOTAL   56690

        GOAL   330000

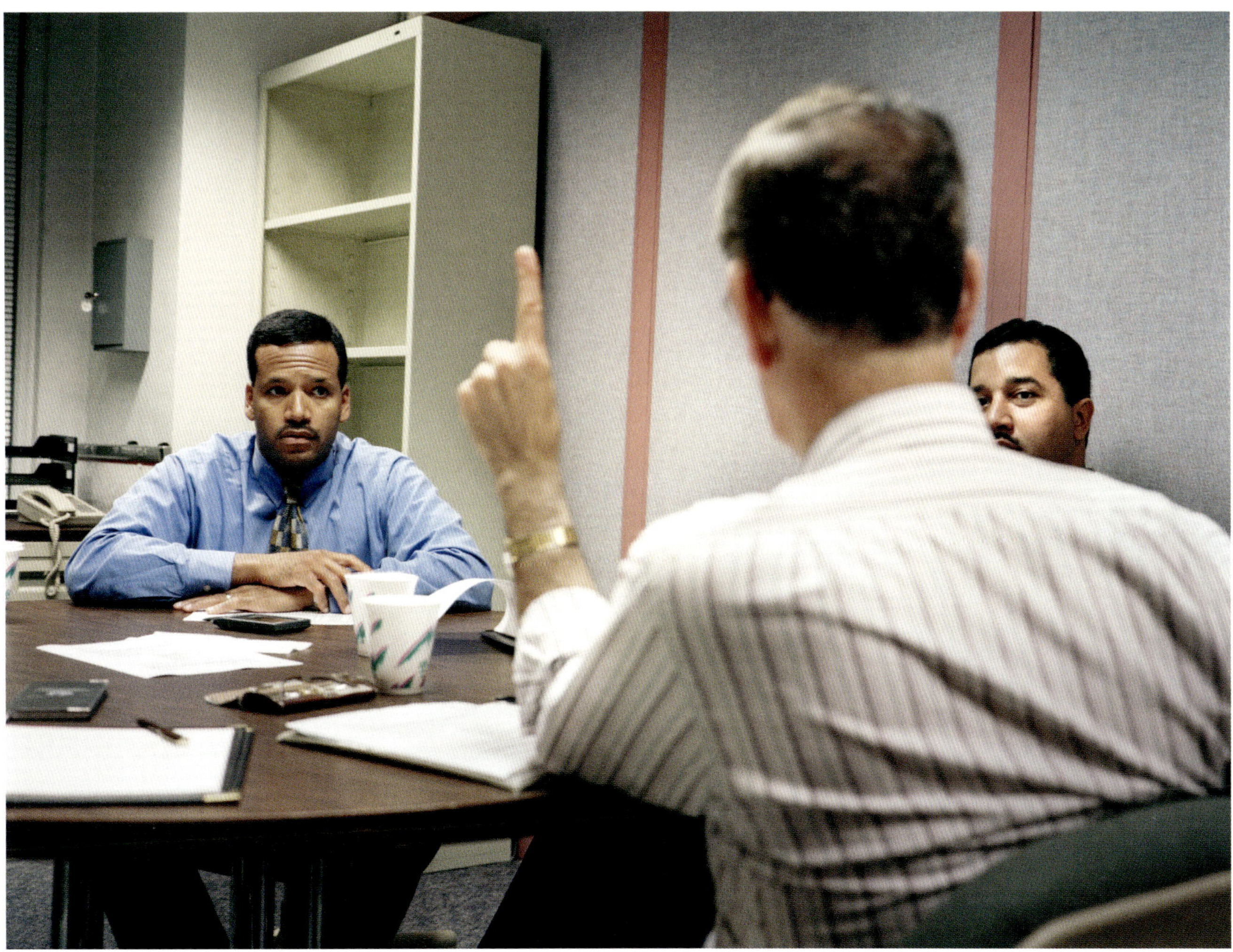

Law Firm

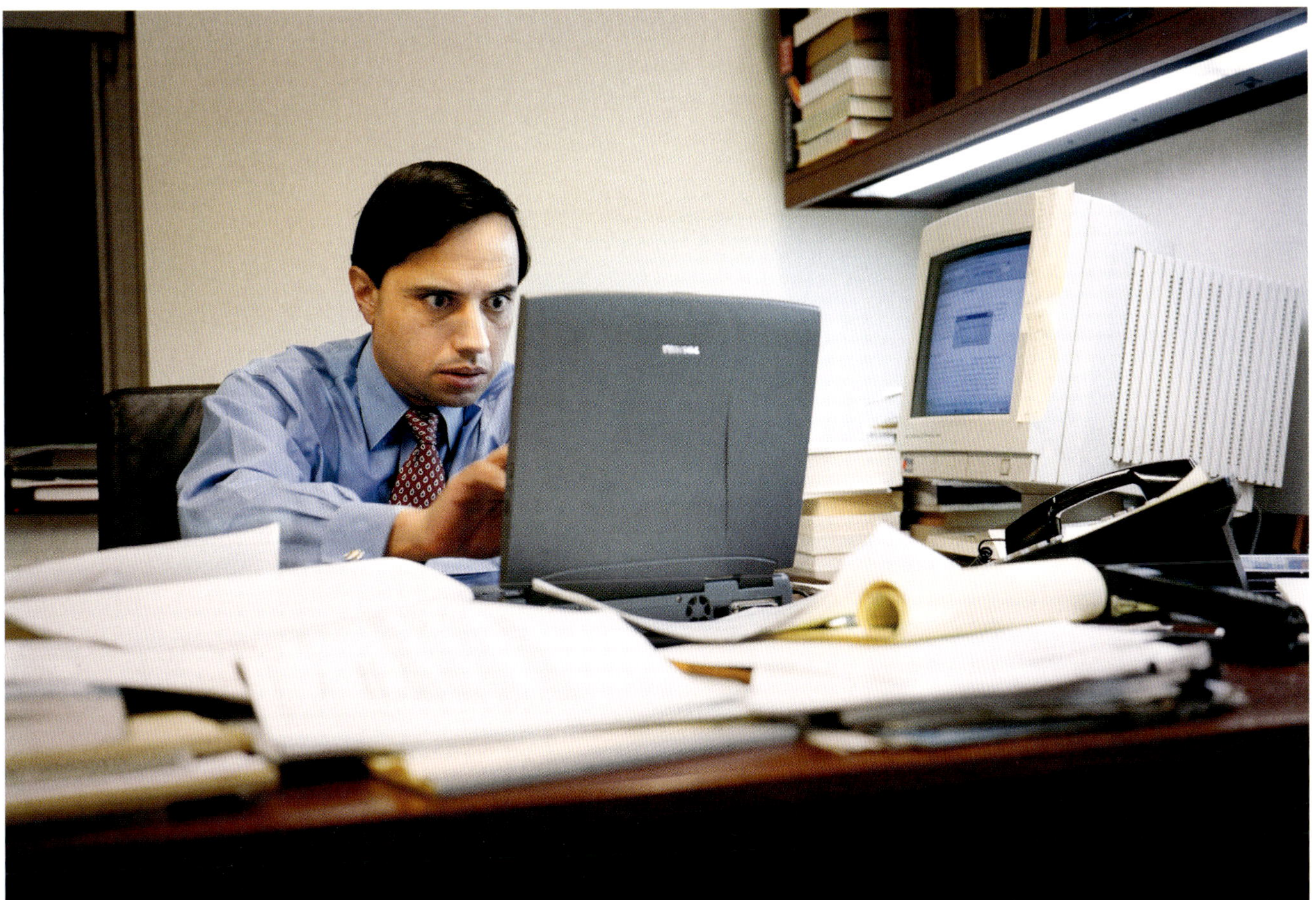

Commercial Bank

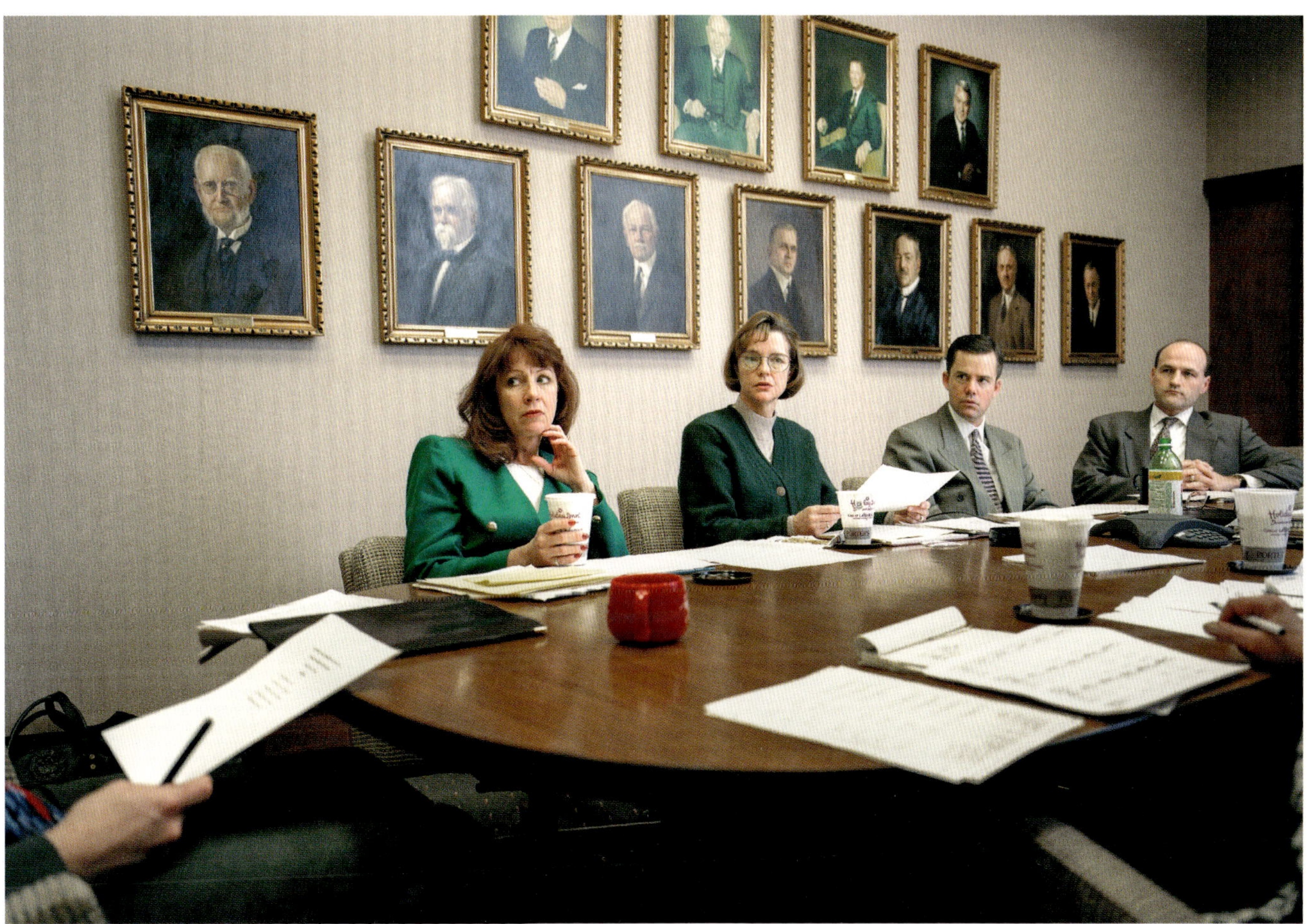

Insurance Company

overleaf: Government Office *(left),* Accounting Firm *(right)*

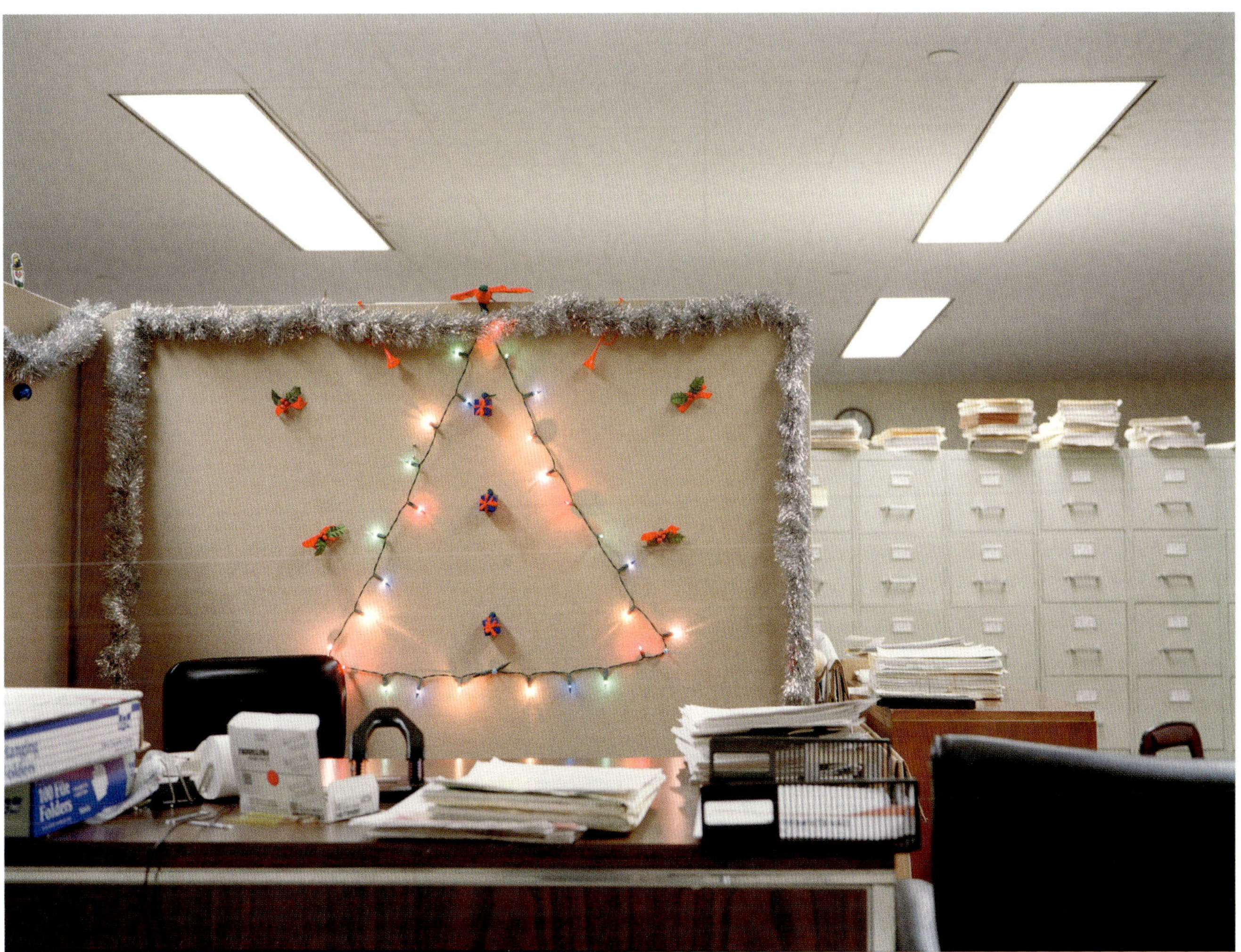

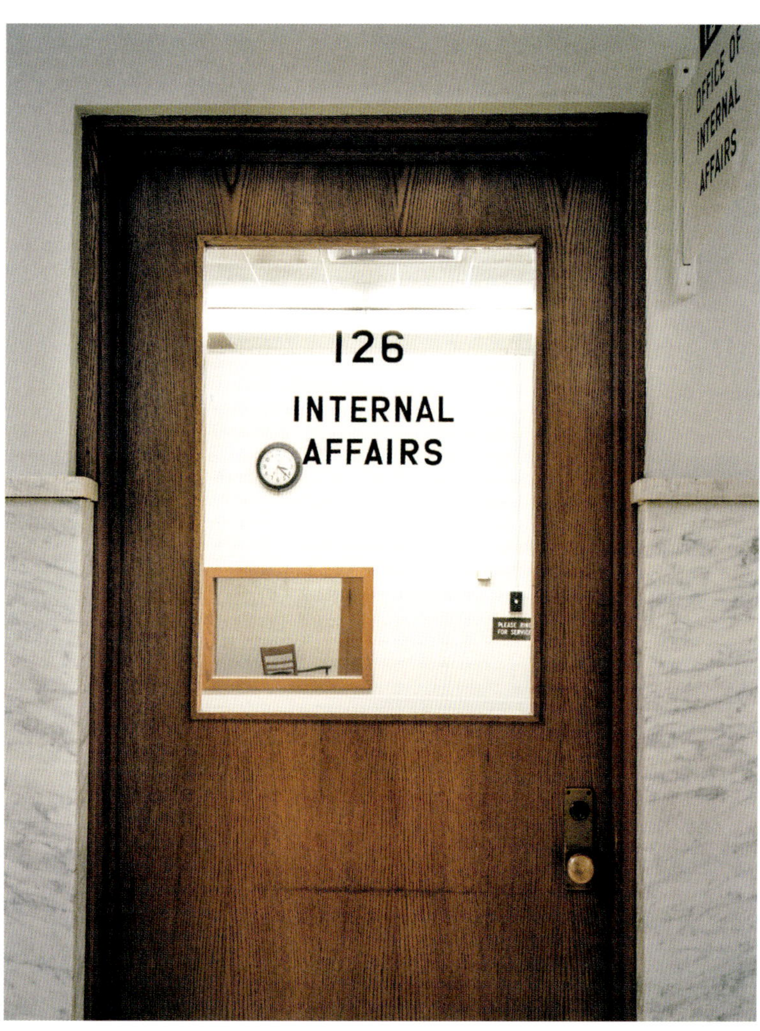

OFFICE OF
INTERNAL
AFFAIRS
126
INTERNAL
AFFAIRS
PLEASE RING
FOR SERVICE

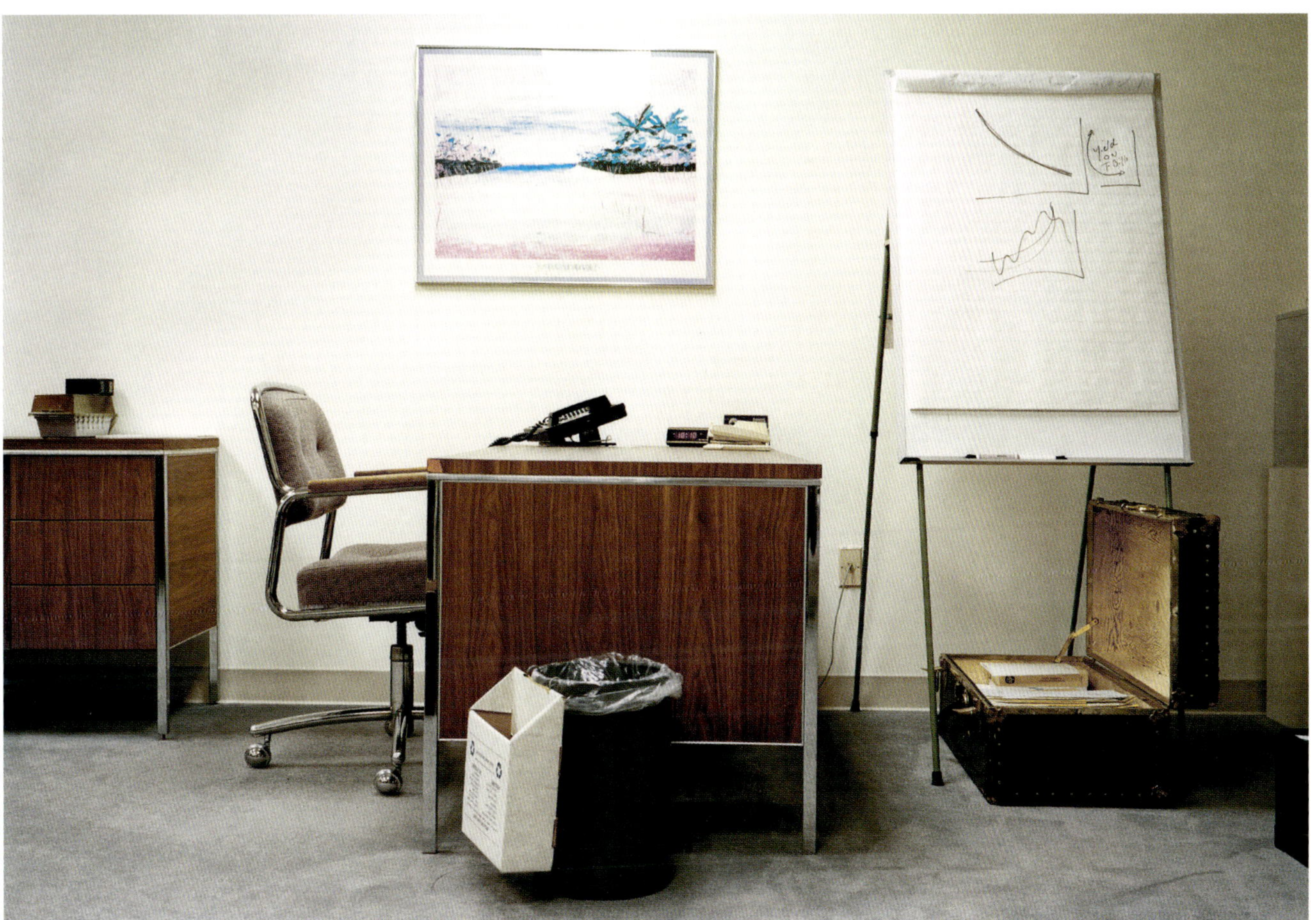

Yield
on
F.D.%

Insurance Company

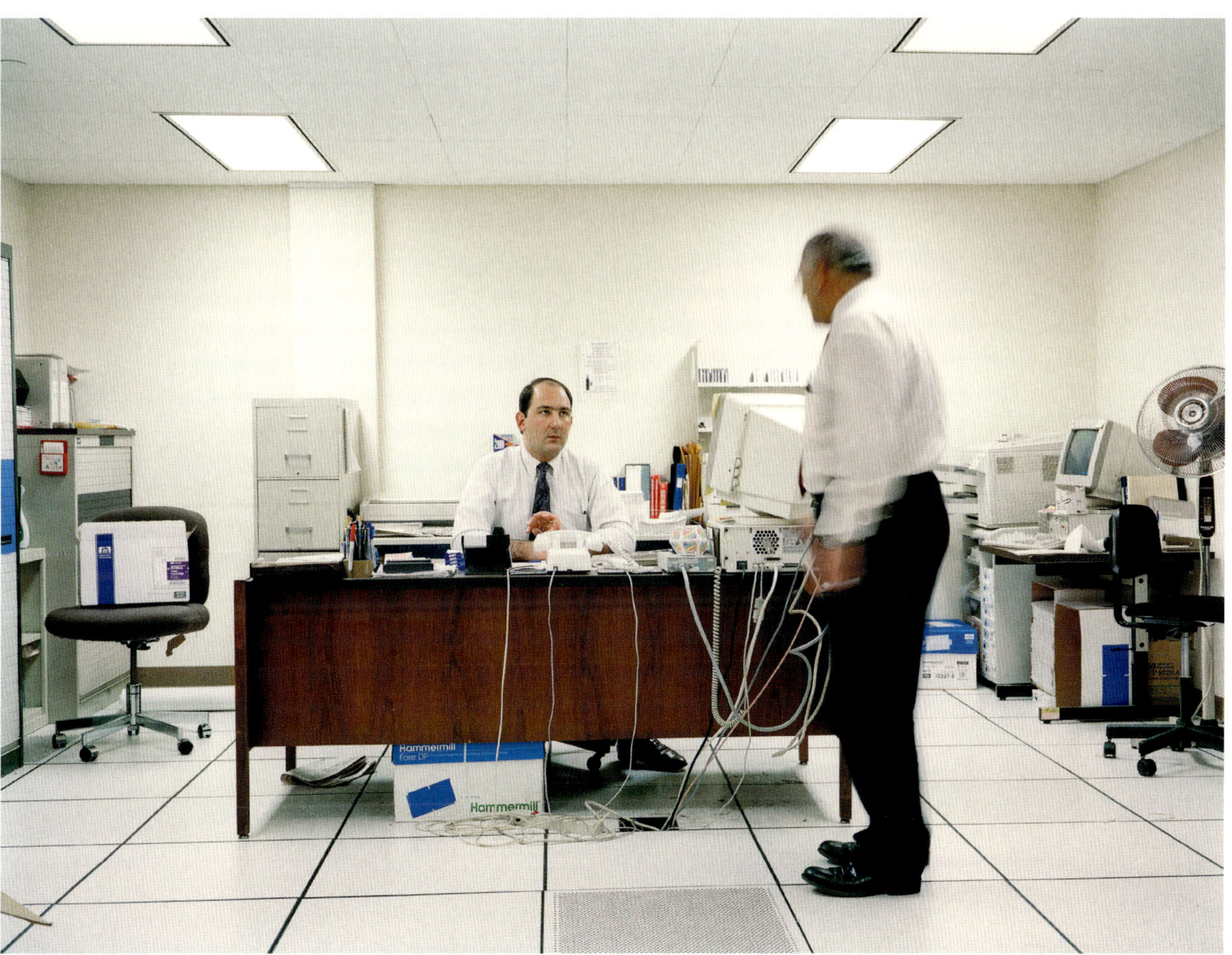

Events Arena

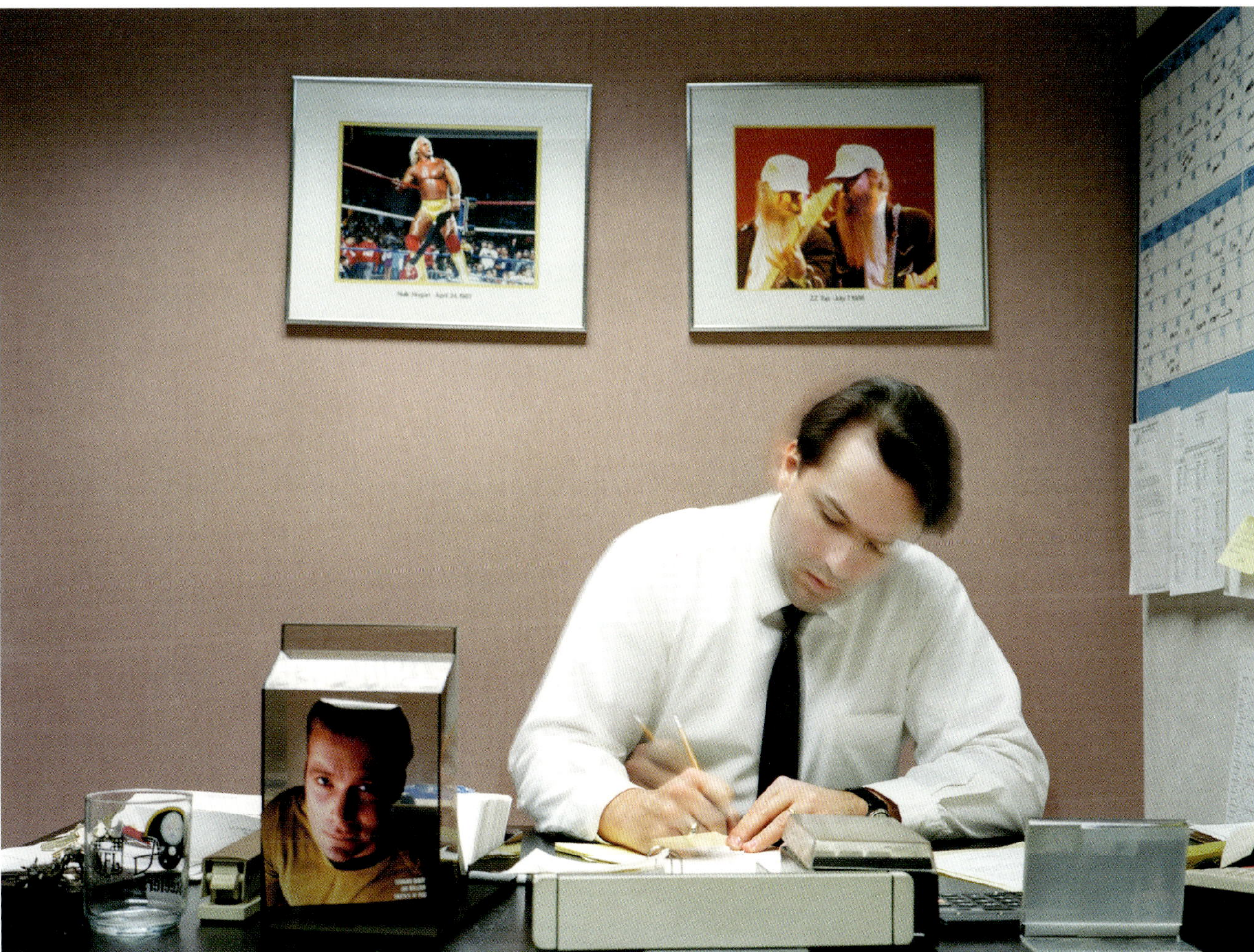

Online Magazine

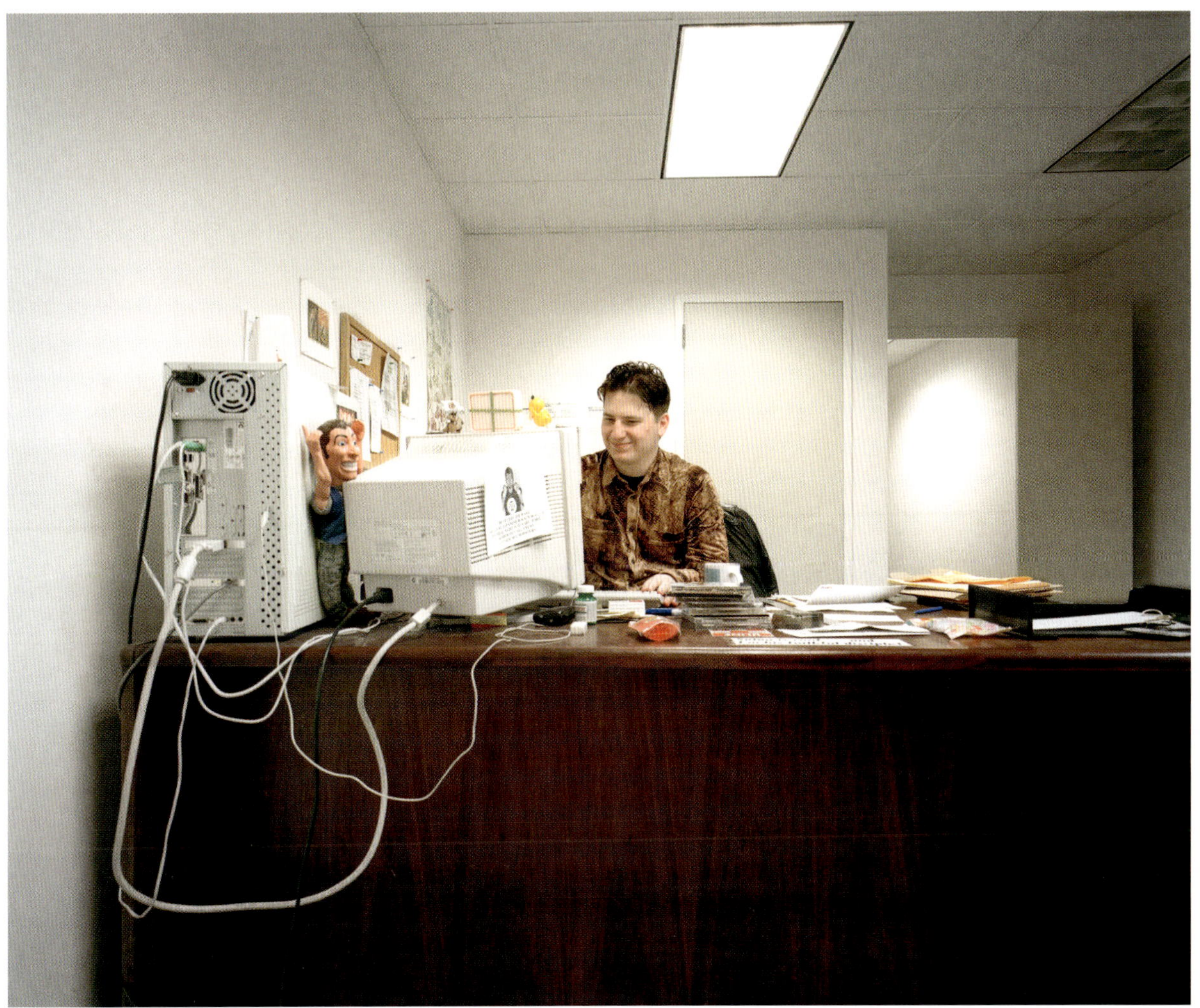

Financial Advisory Firm

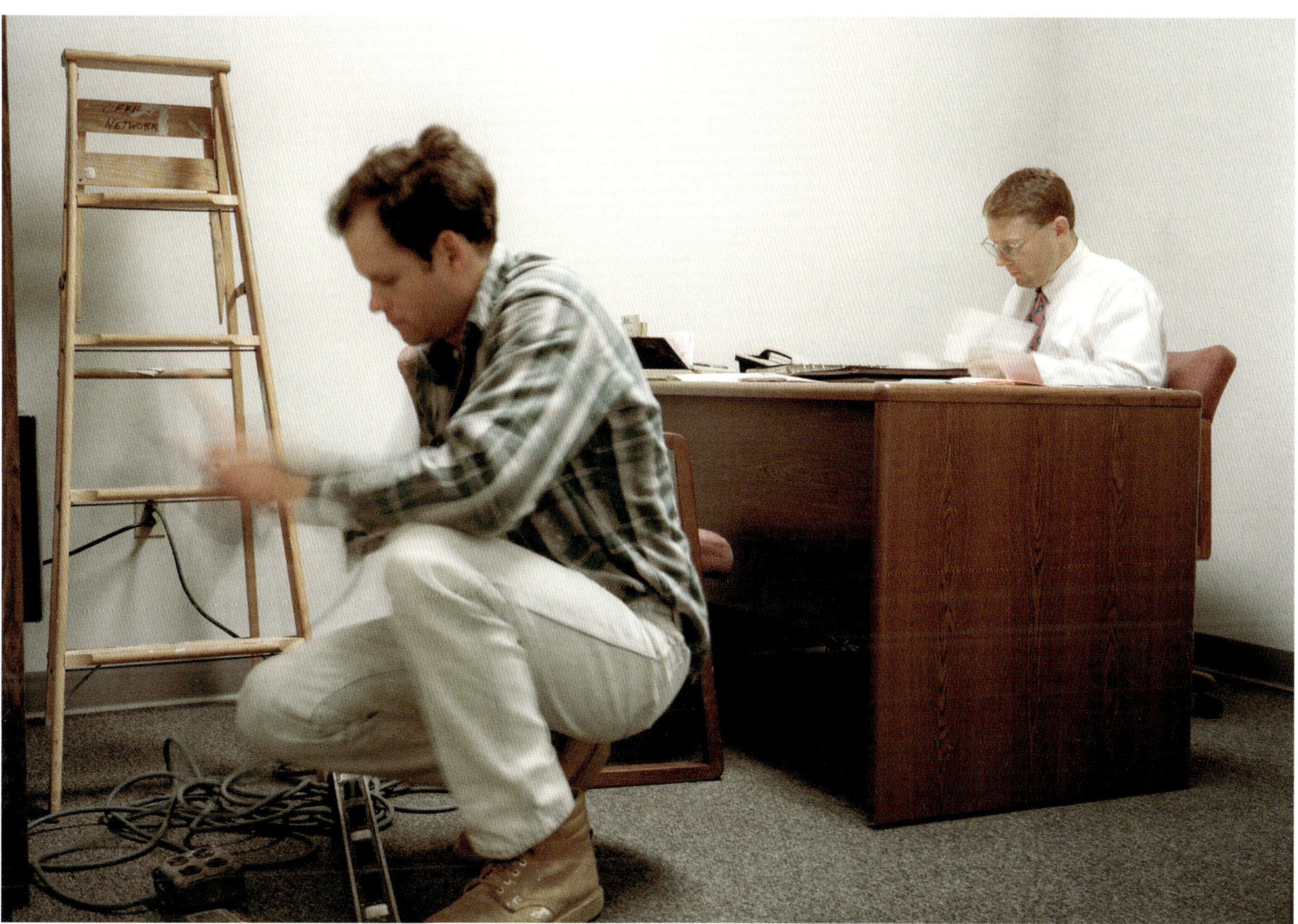
FEI
NETWORK

Commercial Bank

overleaf: Financial Advisory Firm

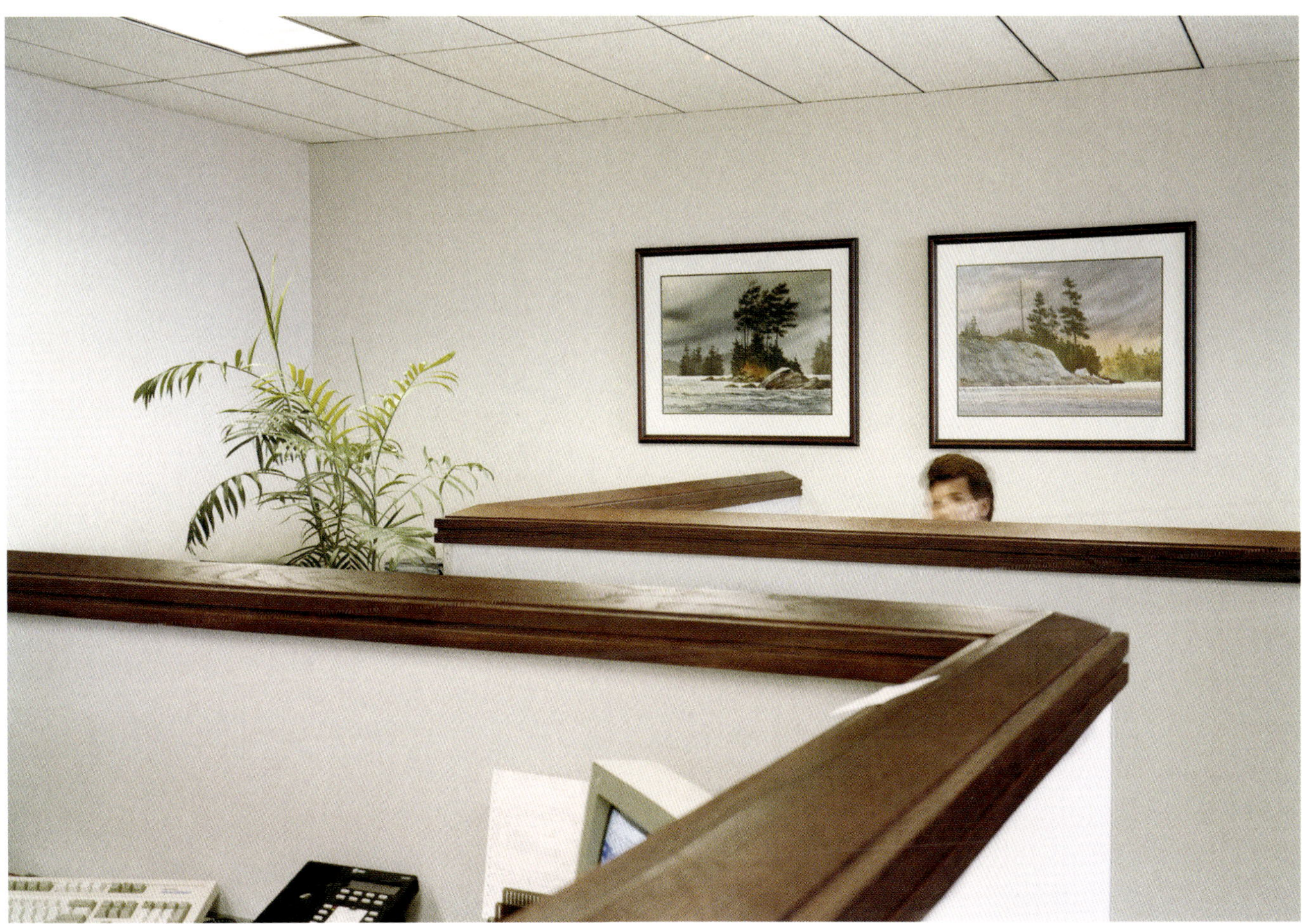

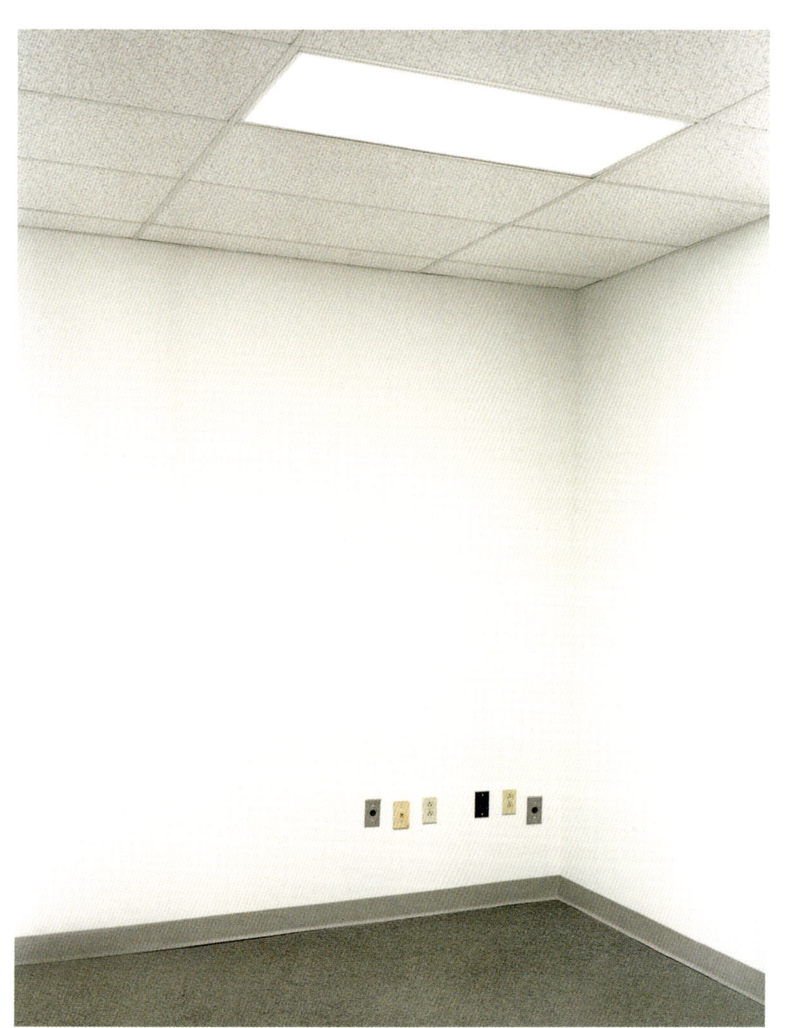

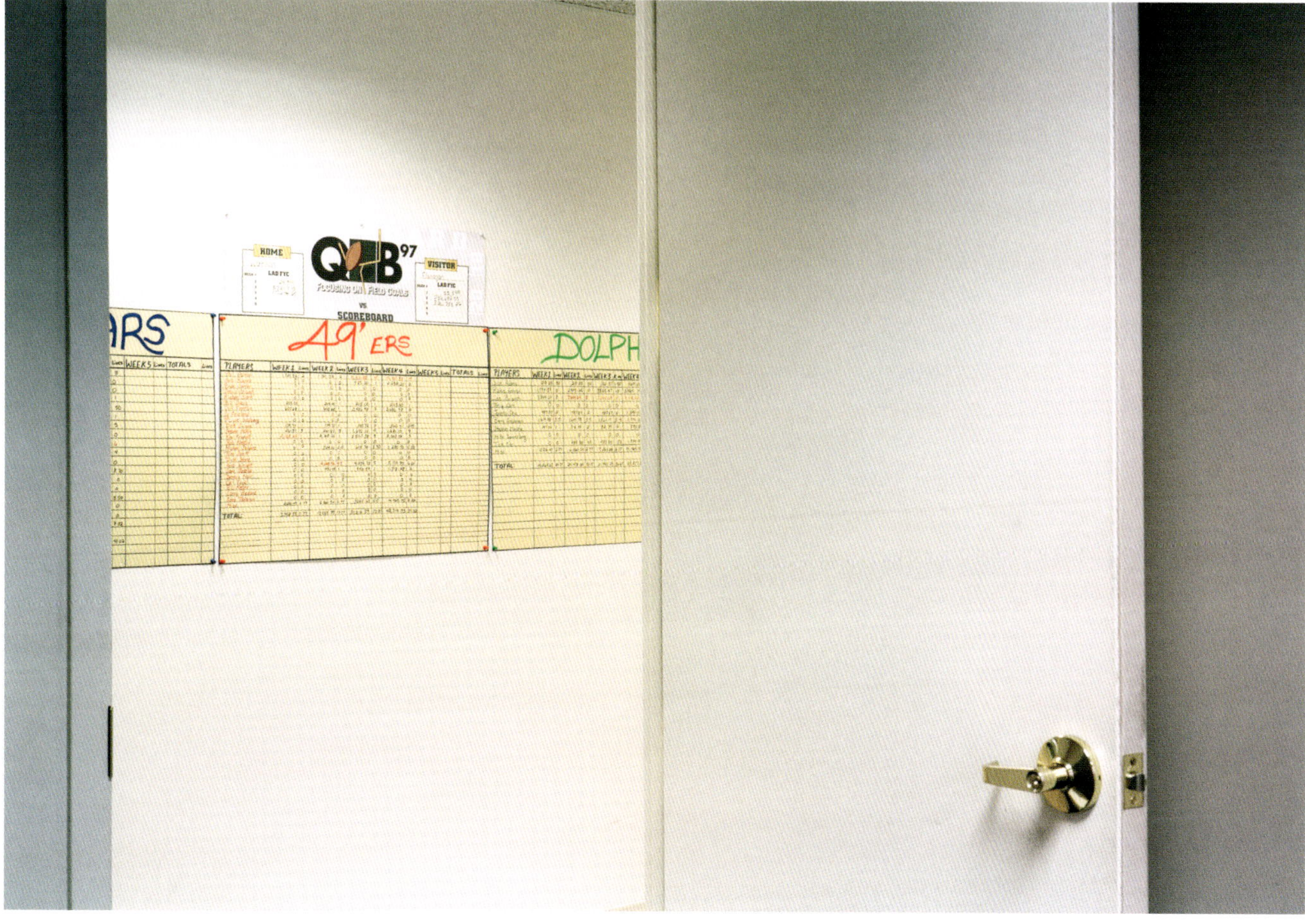
HOME
VISITOR
QB 97
FOCUSING ON FIELD GOALS
SCOREBOARD
ARS
49'ERS
DOLPH

Financial Advisory Firm

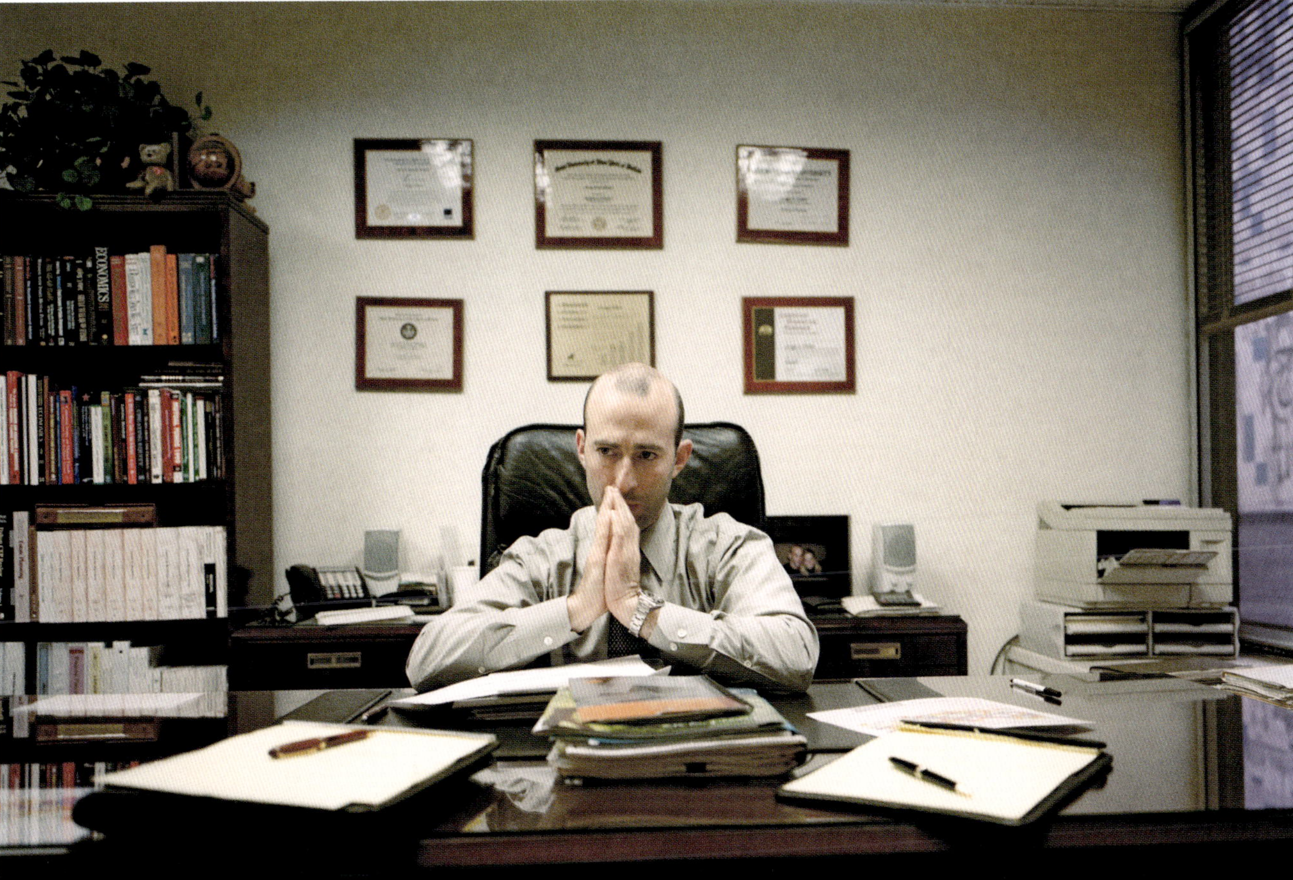

Savings and Loan Company

 Accounting Firm *(left)*, Insurance Company *(right)*

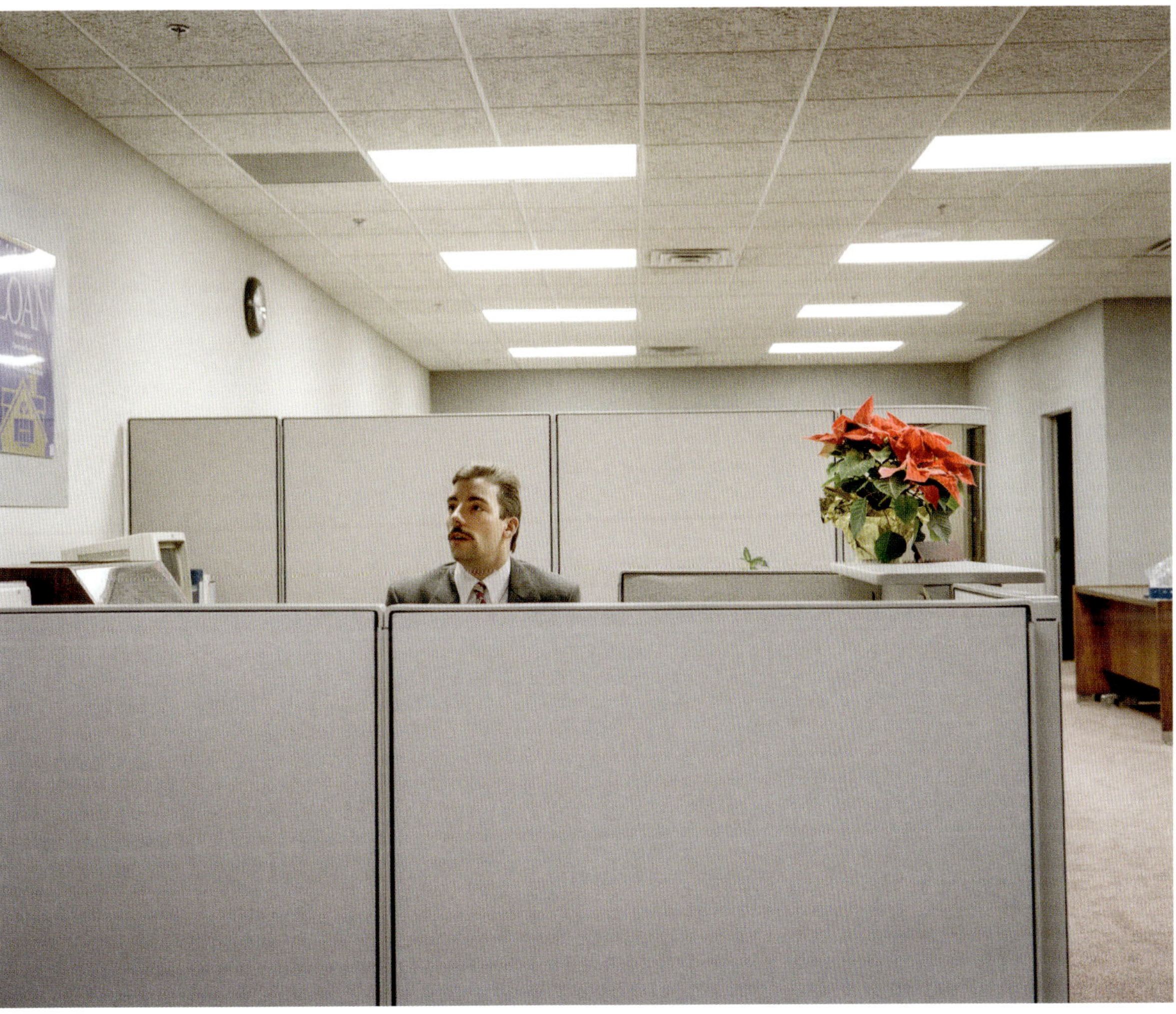

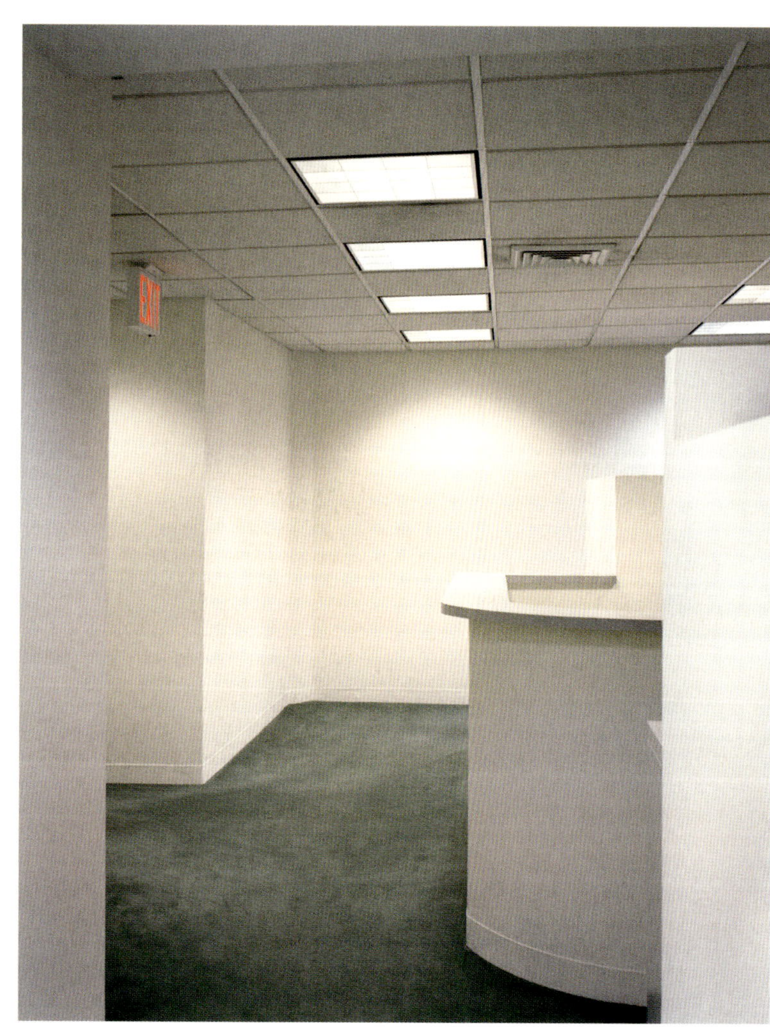

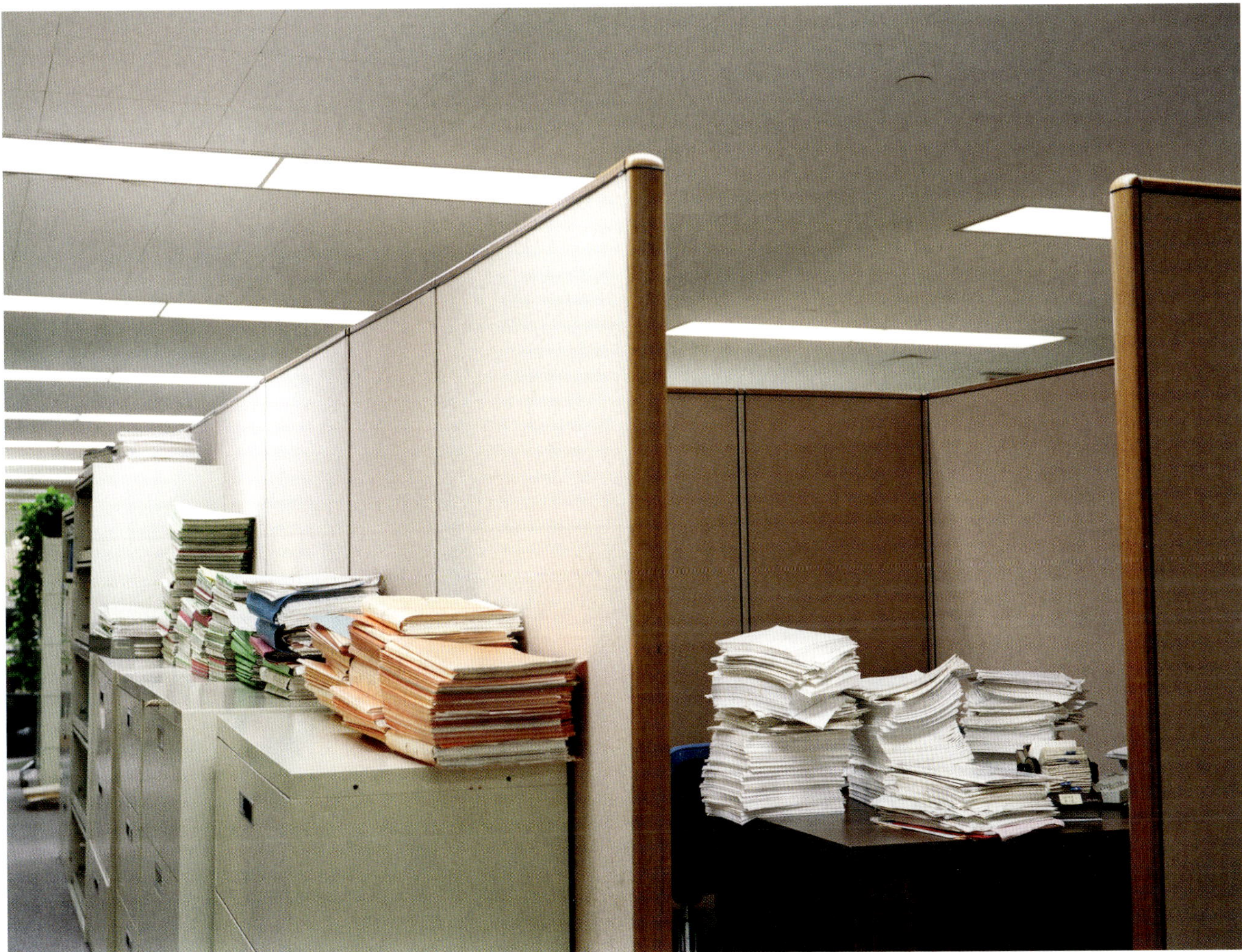

Commercial Bank

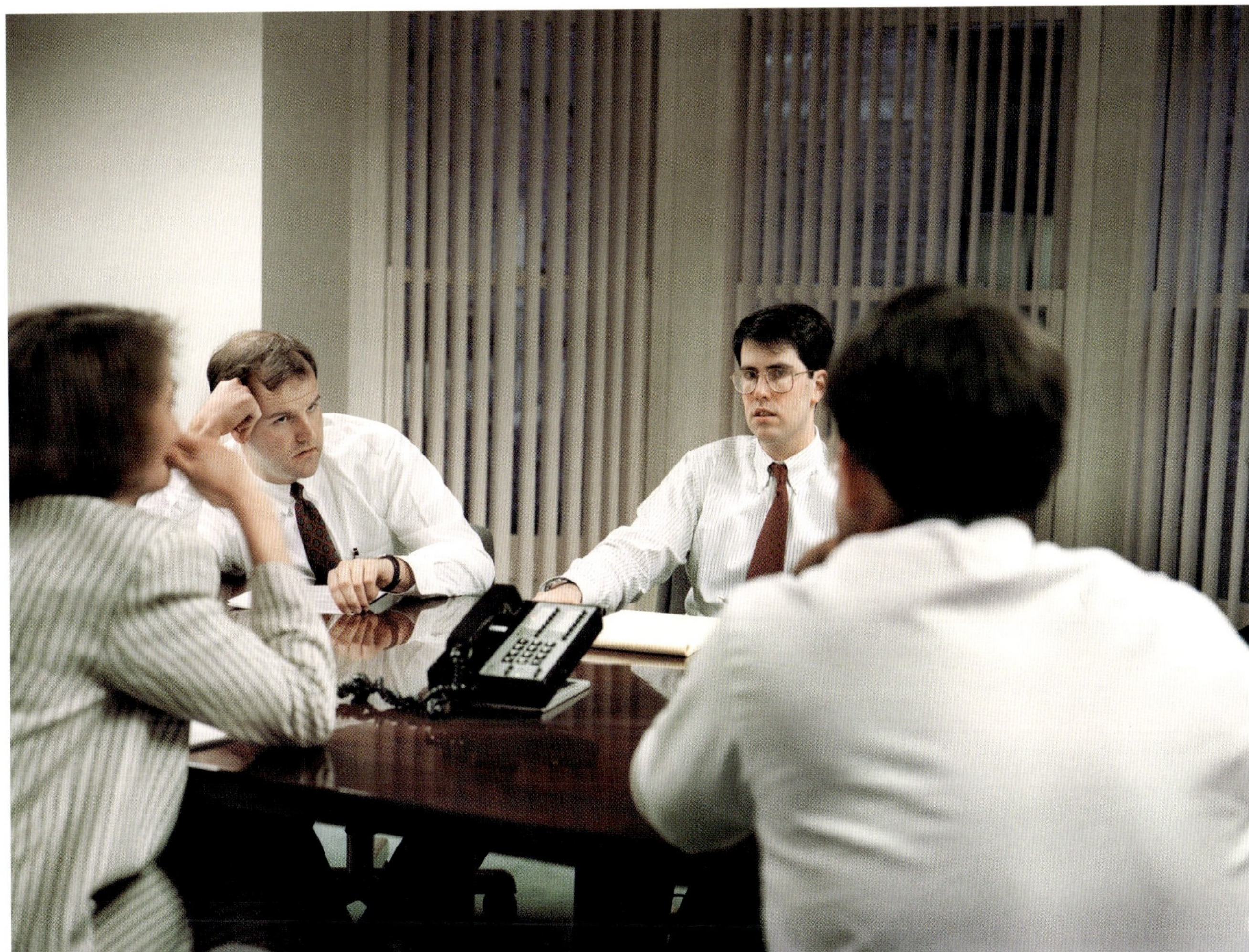

Home Security Company

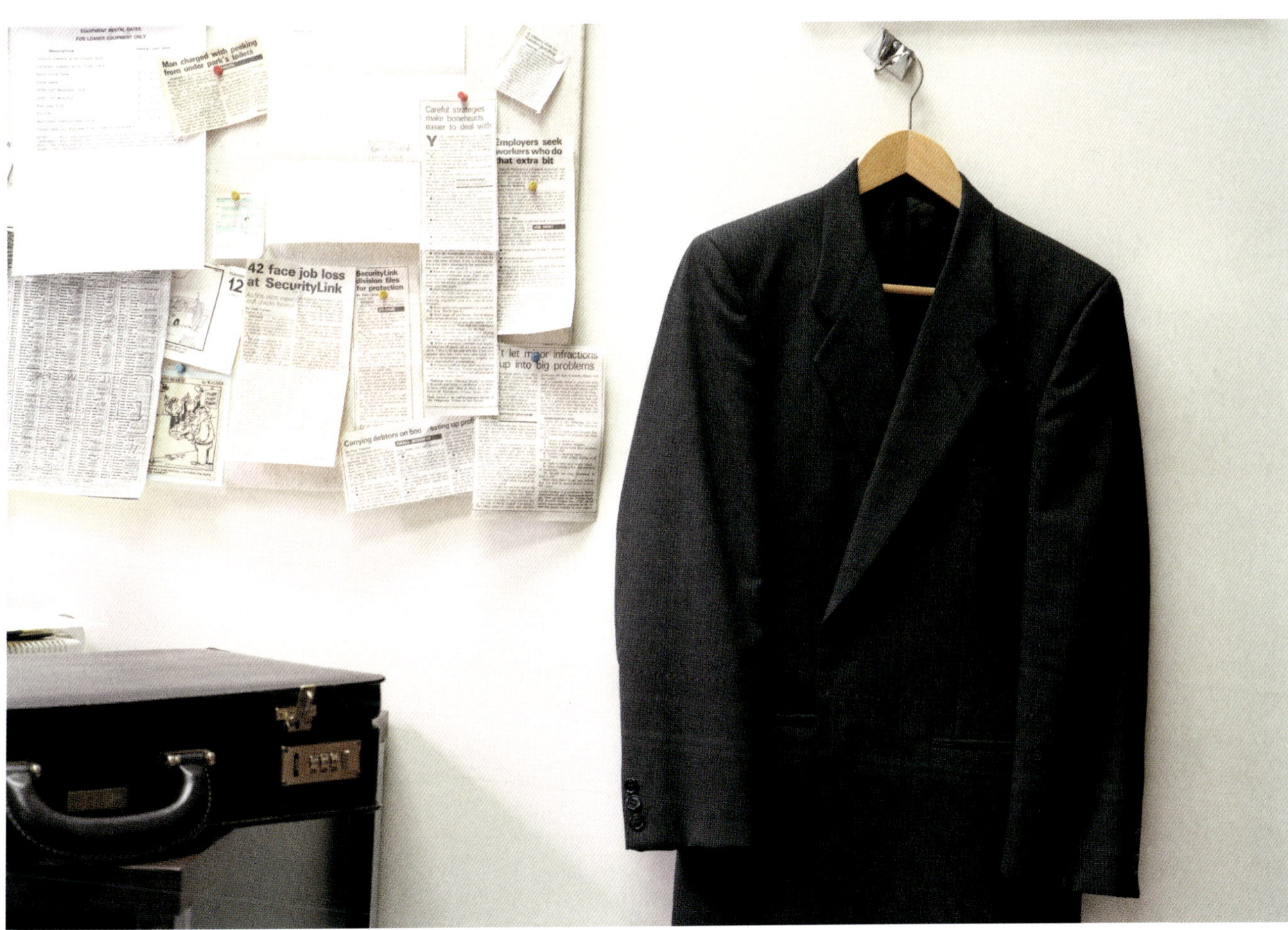

Financial Advisory Firm

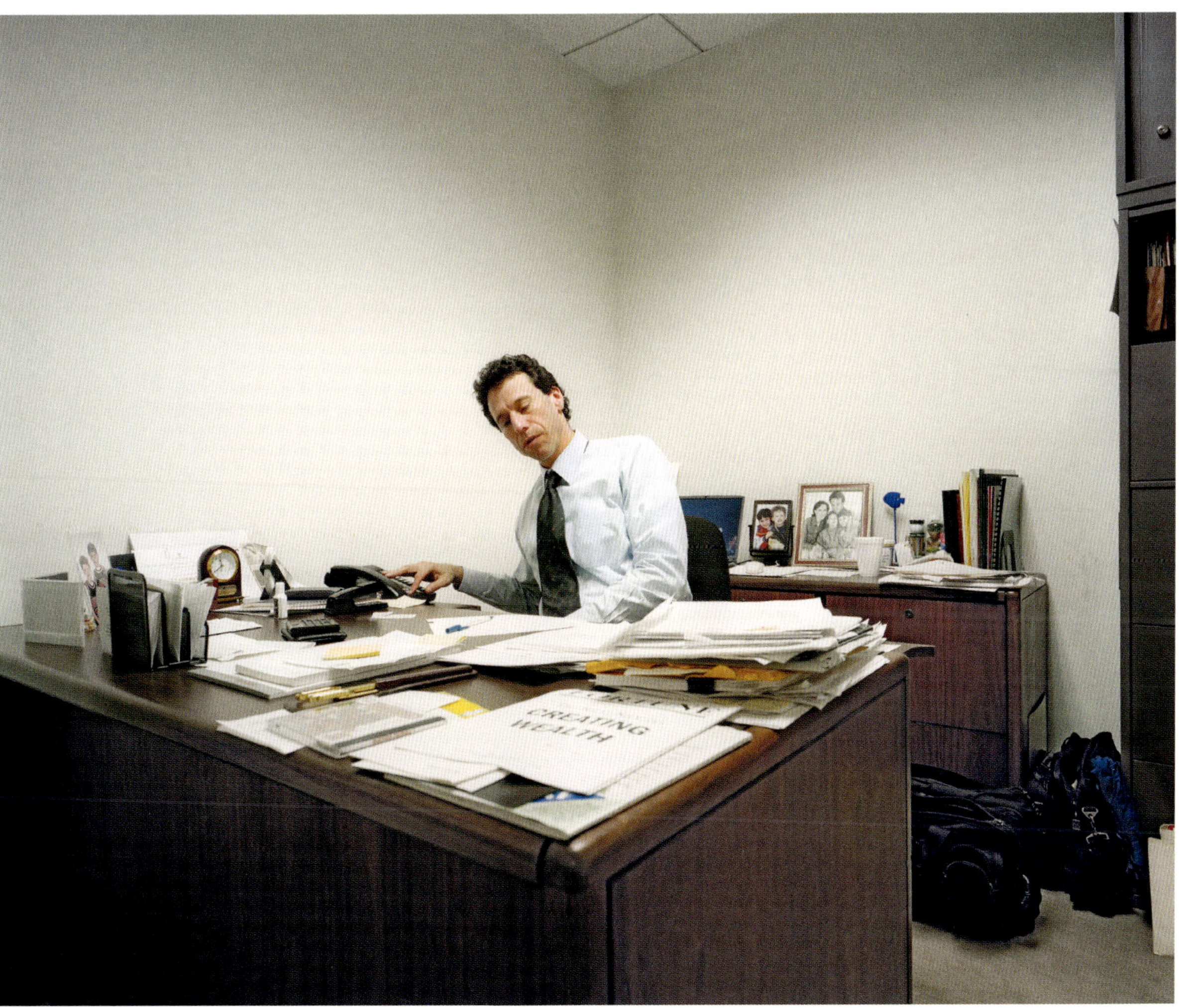

Office Building

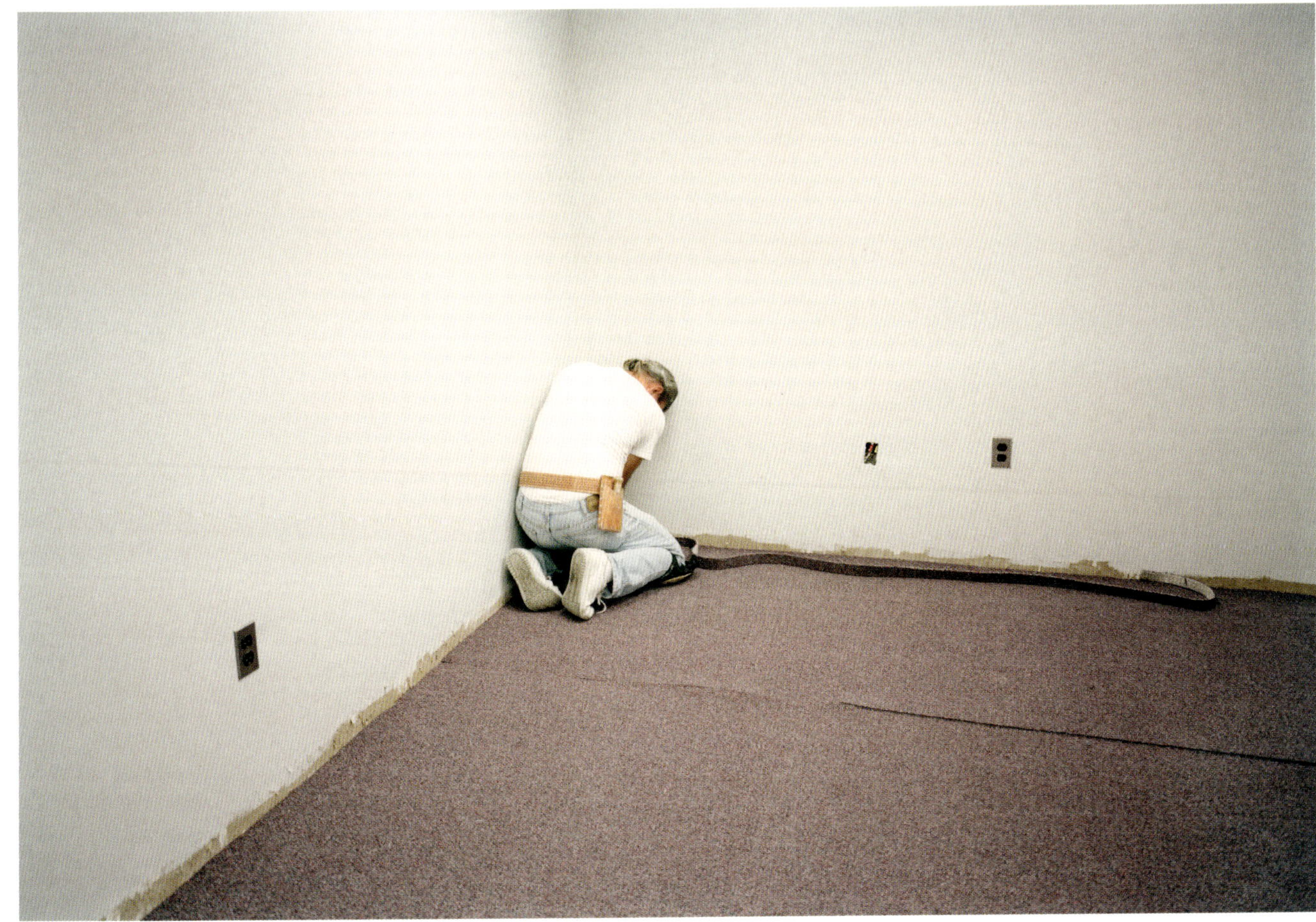

Social Services Office

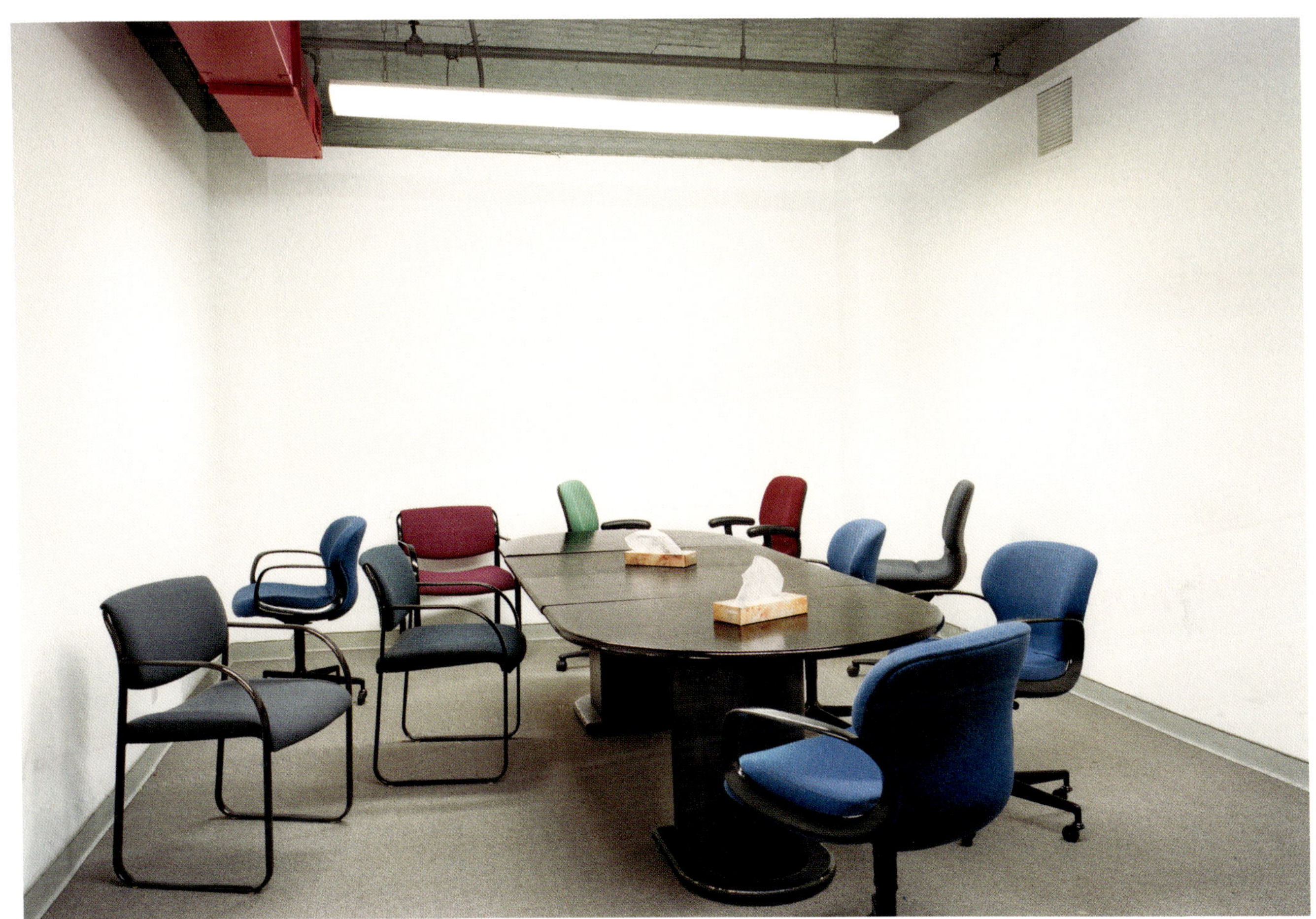

The Office
First edition

Published 2022 by Hoxton Mini Press, London
Copyright © Hoxton Mini Press 2022
All rights reserved

Photographs © Steven Ahlgren
Introduction © Ufrieda Ho
Image layout design and sequence
  by Friederike Huber
Additional design by Daniele Roa
Copy-editing by Florence Filose
Production by Anna De Pascale

Hoxton Mini Press would like to thank
Becca Jones for suggesting this book.

Details of the artwork on page 4 are as follows.
Artist: Hopper, Edward; title: *Office at Night;*
date: 1940; medium: oil on canvas; dimensions:
22–3/16 x 25–1/8" unframed; 30–5/16 x 33–15/16 x
2–3/4" framed. Collection Walker Art Center,
Minneapolis. Gift of the T. B. Walker Foundation,
Gilbert M. Walker Fund, 1948.

ISBN: 978-1-914314-17-9

Printed and bound by Livonia, Latvia

This book is 100% carbon compensated according
to ClimateCalc (climatecalc.eu).
Offset purchased from: Stand For Trees.

For every book you buy from our website,
we plant a tree: www.hoxtonminipress.com